MOTOR RACING'S STRANGEST® RACES

Other titles in the STRANGEST series

Cricket's Strangest Matches
Football's Strangest Matches
Golf's Strangest Rounds
Kent's Strangest Tales
Law's Strangest Cases
London's Strangest Tales
Medicine's Strangest Cases
Rugby's Strangest Matches
Running's Strangest Tales
Shakespeare's Strangest Tales
Teachers' Strangest Tales
Tennis's Strangest Matches

Titles coming soon

Cycling's Strangest Tales
Fishing's Strangest Tales
Horse Racing's Strangest Tales
Sailing's Strangest Tales

MOTOR RACING'S STRANGEST® RACES

Extraordinary but true stories
from over a century of motor racing

GEOFF TIBBALLS

PORTICO

Published in the United Kingdom in 2016 by
Portico
1 Gower Street
London
WC1E 6HD

An imprint of Pavilion Books Company Ltd

ISBN 978-1-91023-296-5

A CIP catalogue record for this book is available from the British Library.

10 9 8 7 6 5 4 3 2 1

Reproduction by Colourdepth UK
Printed and bound by Bookwell, Finland

This book can be ordered direct from the publisher at www.pavilionbooks.com

CONTENTS

INTRODUCTION 10

WORKING UP A HEAD OF STEAM (1894) 13

A MODEST BEGINNING (1895) 16

POLICE BRUTALITY (1898) 19

CHARRON IN REVERSE (1899) 22

THE HOUND FROM HELL (1900) 25

FUELLED BY ALCOHOL (1902) 28

JARROTT'S RUNNING REPAIRS (1902) 30

THE RACE TO DEATH (1903) 34

JOURNEY INTO THE UNKNOWN (1907) 37

THE RACE AROUND THE WORLD (1908) 43

THE FIRING SQUAD (1908) 47

DOGGED BY MISFORTUNE (1912) 50

CHAMPAGNE JULES (1913) 54

ACROSS THE LINE BACKWARDS (1919) 57

A PIT STOP FOR LUNCH (1925) 60

A CLASH OF THE GIANTS (1925) 62

THREE CAR TRICK (1927) 64

THE ACTRESS AND THE OPERA SINGER (1929)   68

THE ICE-MAN MELTETH (1930)   71

FAGIOLI BRINGS THE BRIDGE DOWN (1931)   73

VICTORY AT 1½MPH (1932)   75

CAMPARI'S HAMMER BLOW (1932)   77

A FIERY FINISH (1933)   80

ON THE BEACH (1933)   83

THE FIXED RACE (1933)   85

LE MANS VICTORY SEALED BY CHEWING GUM (1933)   89

THE WRONG PIT SIGNAL (1935)   92

NUVOLARI VERSUS THE GERMANS (1935)   94

AN ENCOUNTER WITH A STAG (1938)   98

THE TIED MONTE (1939)   102

THE WRONG SIDE OF THE ROAD (1940)   104

RACING ON ICE (1947)   107

THE SILVERSTONE SHEEP (1947)   109

FARINA IN A HUFF (1949)   111

CALLED FROM THE BAR (1953)   114

HELL IN BUENOS AIRES (1955)   117

HELPING HANDS (1956)   120

THE DAY THE TRACK MELTED (1959)   124

THE FINAL PUSH (1959)   126

BRABHAM GOES BY TRAM (1960)   129

THE POST-RACE COLLISION (1962)   132

THE GREAT ESCAPE (1965)   134

THE DEMOLITION INDY (1966)   137

A HARE'S BREADTH (1969)   140

ON TOW AROUND MONZA (1969)   142

PUNCH-UP AT THE PALACE (1970)   144

MAD DOGS AND MEXICANS (1970)   147

THE RALLY WITH NO FINISHERS (1972)   149

THROUGH THE BARRICADES (1973)   150

SAFETY FIRST (1973)   153

STUCK IN THE PIT LANE (1974)   156

HALF POINTS IN BARCELONA (1975)   158

VICTORY IN SLOW MOTION (1976)   161

SIX WHEELS ON MY WAGON (1976)   163

HUNT'S FLAG DAY (1976)   165

LAUDA SURRENDERS THE TITLE (1976)   168

FAN WORSHIP (1978)   172

AN UNEXPECTED OBSTRUCTION (1979)   174

THE RACE THAT NEVER WAS (1980)   176

MANSELL: A PAINFUL BEGINNING (1980)   179

THE LONG WAIT (1981)   182

A FALLING-OUT AMONG FRIENDS (1982)   184

ALL CHANGE AT MONACO (1982)   187

A HINT OF NATIONAL BIAS? (1982)   189

IT'S A WASHOUT (1986)   192

A FAMILY AFFAIR (1988)   195

THE BATTLE OF SUZUKA (1990)   198

THE 25-MINUTE GRAND PRIX (1991)   201

MANSELL AND THE SAFETY TRUCK (1993)   203

THE RACE AGAINST THE TRAIN (1993)   206

LET THE SUNSHINE IN (1996)   208

ROAD RAGE (1997)   210

AFTER YOU, MIKA! (1998)   213

SCHUMACHER WINS IN THE PITS (1998)   216

CARNAGE AT LA SOURCE (1998)   219

THE SHED, THE BED AND THE BOOT (1999)   223

NO TYRES FOR IRVINE (1999)   225

THE SIX-DAY WORLD CHAMPION (1999)   229

COULTHARD AND THE TRESPASSER (2000)   232

THE UGLY SIX PACK (2005)   235

FORTY-ONE PEOPLE WENT TO MOW (2006)   239

A PASSAGE THROUGH INDIA (2006)   242

THE DELIBERATE CRASH (2008)   245

FINAL TURN DECIDER (2008)   248

LAST TO FIRST (2011)   251

THIS LITTLE PIGGY (2014)   253

A CRAZY MISCALCULATION (2015)   255

My first priority is to finish above, rather than beneath, the ground.

(James Hunt, 1947–93)

INTRODUCTION

When the motley assortment of steam and petrol-powered vehicles lined up in Paris in 1894 at the start of the trial to Rouen, they launched the colourful history of motor racing. Many of the pioneering events were death-defying, trans-continental marathons, occasionally visiting remote settlements that had never before seen a motor car, in which the competitors were obliged to negotiate basic dirt tracks, muddy bogs, fast-flowing rivers, over-zealous policemen and a seemingly endless supply of stray dogs.

France led the way, not only in *chiens perdus*, but also in promoting the sport of motor racing. One of many ingenious events was an 1899 handicap race between walkers, horsemen, cycles, motorcycles and cars over the 104 miles (167km) between Paris and Trouville. The horses were allotted 14 hours and finished first and second; the cars, allowed three hours, were third and fourth. The walkers are probably still out there somewhere.

Meanwhile the United States specialised in endurance contests, some of which were highly charged affairs. In 1902 one John Grant Lyman was suspended for six months by the Automobile Club of America for the heinous crime of exceeding 20mph (32.2km/h) during the Long Island Endurance Run.

The first regular circuit race, the Circuit des Ardennes, took place in 1902 but it was several years before this type of event became popular. And in those days a lap could be anything up to 75 miles (121km) – as in Germany's Kaiserpreis – and take the best part of an hour and a half. Spectator satisfaction was not exactly high on the list of priorities.

Since these humble beginnings, the human race has done many strange things to motor cars in the name of sport – some barely legal. Cars have been bullied and coerced in a manner which would make even Basil Fawlty blush and have taken part in events best classified as innovative. How else would you describe a race where a four-poster bed chases a garden shed around a Grand Prix circuit?

Gathered here are races with strange beginnings, strange middle bits and strange finishes, as well as races which were just ... strange. They include the Frenchman who drove 25 miles (40.2km) in reverse; the Grand Prix where the leading drivers were so far ahead that they stopped for a meal in the pits; the Le Mans 24-Hour Race won by a car patched up with chewing gum; and the driver who drank six bottles of champagne – virtually one per pit stop – on the way to winning the Indianapolis 500. Most of the great names are featured as sometimes willing, sometimes baffled, participants – Boillot, Nuvolari, Varzi, Farina, Fangio, Moss, Brabham, Stewart, Hunt, Mansell, Senna, Schumacher and Hamilton.

For the purposes of this book, I have included a few memorable rallies, too, partly because rallies are races in all but name and also because their catalogues of incomprehensible rules and regulations lend themselves to the bizarre. A race against time which ends with a stage to see who can go the slowest really does defy description! Yet that was precisely what the organisers of the Monte Carlo Rally came up with in 1932.

Dick Dastardly and Muttley would have loved every minute!

A big thank you to the following for making hours of

research so rewarding: The British Newspaper Library, Nottinghamshire Library Services, Westminster Library, Marylebone Library, Derby City Library, Sheffield Library, Southport Local Studies Library, Donington Park race track and the *Derby Evening Telegraph*. Thanks also to Nicola Newman at Portico and Katie Hewett, and to Jeremy Robson for giving the original project the green light.

Geoff Tibballs

WORKING UP A HEAD OF STEAM

PARIS TO ROUEN TRIAL, 22 JULY 1894

Motoring was still very much in its infancy when Pierre Giffard, editor and owner of the Parisian newspaper *Le Petit Journal*, hit upon the idea of staging the world's first motor event. It was not a race as such but an 80 mile (129km) trial along the bumpy roads between Paris and Rouen, the winner to be the vehicle which, in the opinion of the judges (all of whom were on the staff of *Le Petit Journal*) most closely adhered to their ideal of *'d'être sans danger, aisément maniable pour les voyagers, et de ne pas coûter trop cher sur la route'*, in other words safe, easy to handle and cheap to run. Hoping for a large turn-out to ensure maximum publicity for his newspaper, M. Giffard was no doubt heartened to receive entries from 102 drivers putting their names forward to compete for the handsome first prize of 5,000 francs. The entry list contained a vast array of vehicles, hardly any two alike, and featuring no fewer than 20 different methods of propulsion. These ranged from the more conventional steam-powered designs or the new-fangled petrol-powered cars to contraptions driven by compressed air, clockwork, gravity, a system of pendulums, 'a combination of animate and mechanical motor' and even the rocket-like Baricycle, a device which was propelled solely by the weight of its passengers!

The organisers laid down strict regulations governing which vehicles would actually be allowed to compete. First there was an inspection test which eliminated all but 25 of the original 102, principally the more bizarre entries. The event itself was scheduled for 7 June but with a number of vehicles still not ready by the start of that month, it was postponed until 22 July. This allowed more opportunity to arrange a 32 mile (51.4km) qualifying trial, which every competitor had to pass. The time limit set was three hours, thus necessitating an average speed of just over 10mph (16.1km/h), but this was deemed too harsh and so the time was extended to four hours, thereby reducing the required speed to a more attainable 8mph (12.9km/h). Seventeen vehicles took part in the first qualifying run on 19 July, but only 13 passed. A second run on the twentieth saw all six starters pass and two more qualified the following day, to leave a starting line-up of 21 (all powered by either petrol or steam engines) for the journey to Rouen.

The festivities began at 8a.m. in the Paris suburb of Neuilly and the route ran via Nanterre, St Germain, Mantes (where drivers would stop for lunch) and Vernon to Rouen. Along the way entire villages turned out to cheer and to shower the vehicles with flowers and fruit. Families set up picnic tables at the side of the road so that they could gawp at the great monsters as they trundled by. For some, it would be the first time they had ever seen a motor car. On board each car, in addition to the driver and passenger, was an official observer to determine whether the criteria for the first prize were met. The vehicles were flagged off at 30-second intervals, but it soon became apparent that the most powerful vehicle by far was a giant De Dion articulated steam tractor driven by wealthy playboy and renowned duellist Count Jules de Dion. The leaders covered the 30 miles (48.3km) to Mantes by 11a.m., de Dion showing the way to Georges Lemaître in a Peugeot and Emile Levassor in a Panhard. The attempts at official timekeeping at Mantes were singularly chaotic, but after a leisurely lunch, the drivers began the second leg of their journey at 1.30p.m.

It came as no surprise that Count de Dion maintained his lead all the way to Rouen. He had the odd hair-raising moment along the way, once having to be hauled free by spectators after his vehicle became stuck on the road's loose stone surface, and on another occasion taking a wrong turning and ending up in a potato field. He finished in 6hr 48min at a commendable average speed of 11⅔mph (18.8km/h), three and a half minutes ahead of Lemaître. However, the Count did not win the coveted first prize, the judges ruling that because it needed two people to handle it – a driver to steer and a stoker to tend the engine – the De Dion tractor did not comply with the event's aims. Therefore he was demoted to second although he was praised for his 'interesting steam tractor which … develops a speed absolutely beyond comparison, especially when going uphill'. Instead the prize was awarded jointly to Lemaître and Levassor for their petrol cars. Indeed the day was a triumph for the brash new petrol machines. For while all 13 petrol-powered cars completed the course, four of the eight steam-powered vehicles broke down. For reliability, it was clear that the future of motoring lay with petrol.

A MODEST BEGINNING

CHICAGO EXHIBITION RUN, 28 NOVEMBER 1895

Judging from the widespread apathy on display at America's first organised race, it must have been hard to believe that motoring would ever catch on in that country. Competitors and spectators alike seemed distinctly underwhelmed by the prospect of a 94 mile (151km) round trip from Chicago to Waukegan, with the result that the victorious vehicle in this trailblazing event returned home to little more than polite applause from a handful of hardy souls.

The competition was modelled on the Paris-Rouen Trial, coverage of which had been relayed to the United States by an enthusiastic young *New York Herald* reporter who followed the drivers part of the way through France on a bicycle. His reports of the adventurers across the Atlantic and of the thousands of people who had turned out to watch spurred American newspapers to attempt something similar. The American counterpart was sponsored by the *Chicago Times-Herald,* and 2 November was set aside for what promised to be one of the most exciting spectacles to grace the city all year. The omens appeared good when over 100 entries were received, but come the day of the 'exhibition run', as it was called, only two turned up – a Duryea Motor Wagon, driven by Frank Duryea, and a Mueller-Benz, driven by the designer's son, Oscar Mueller. This was not exactly the grand pageant that the organisers had in mind. In a decidedly low-key affair, the pair set off from 55th Street on their journey to Waukegan, but, if possible, the finish was even less impressive than the start. For the Duryea broke down, allowing Mueller to come home in splendid isolation and win the reduced prize of $500 which was awarded just for finishing.

The event was such a disappointment that the organisers decided to try again and rescheduled it for 28 November. This time six cars – four petrol and two electric – were set to start before once again fate took a hand, this time in the shape of the weather. Blizzard conditions had deposited 2ft (0.6m) of snow on parts of the city, forcing the route to be shortened to 54 miles (86.9km) – to Evanston and back. Worse still, one of the entries, a de la Vergne-Benz, became stuck in the slush on the way to the start at Jackson Park and had to withdraw. So just five started – Duryea and Mueller again, a Morris and Slalom electric car, a Sturges electric motorcycle, and a Macy-Benz. It was Jerry O'Connor in the Macy-Benz who set the pace, despite an unfortunate incident when he hit a horse-drawn bus, slid over a railroad track and collided with a sleigh carrying journalists. Happily nobody was injured but the Benz's steering was never quite the same after that. Nevertheless, O'Connor still led Duryea by two minutes at the Evanston turning point. However, on the homeward journey the steering deteriorated to such an extent that he had to retire. This left the way – if not the road – clear for Duryea, profiting from the ingenuity of his brother Charles who used a horse-drawn sleigh to service the car.

Back in Jackson Park, Chicago, the crowd were growing restless. They'd had enough after nearly eight hours of standing in the bitter cold and when dusk arrived with still no sign of the cars, they began to drift home. By the time Duryea eventually arrived, there were barely 50 people to see him cross the finish line. He covered the distance in 8hr 23min at an average speed of just over 6mph (9.7km/h), his efforts earning him the full first prize of $2,000. Nearly half an hour later, the only other finisher, the Mueller-Benz, rumbled into the park, with the race umpire, Charles King, doing the steering. He was using one hand to steer the car and the other to prop up the miserable Mueller, who had collapsed from exposure. All in all, it was an inauspicious climax to a somewhat unsatisfactory event. For American motor sport things could only get better – and fortunately they did.

POLICE BRUTALITY
PARIS-AMSTERDAM-PARIS,
7 JULY 1898

While the Americans were still fighting shy of motoring,
the French had embraced it with open arms. France was
the only country with a network of half-decent roads,
the rest of the world having to make do with dusty tracks
which deteriorated into mud pools when it rained.
Encouraged by the wave of enthusiasm from the French
public, the Automobile Club de France announced the first
international race, to go from France through Belgium, on
to Holland and back. The Paris-Amsterdam-Paris event
was eagerly anticipated by almost everyone ... except for
a Monsieur Bochet, the chief engineer of the Paris police.

Bochet was concerned about the safety aspect following
two deaths in the Course de Périgueux which had been
staged two months earlier in the south-west of the country.
So as the start for the Paris-Amsterdam-Paris race drew
near, he informed the ACF that under an obscure local
by-law which he had unearthed, all of the competing cars
would first have to be issued with a certificate stating that
they were safe to be driven on public roads. To obtain the
necessary certificate, they would have to submit to a personal
inspection from him. When the drivers duly presented their
cars for inspection, he took great delight in rejecting the vast
majority. Outraged by this interference, the drivers declared
their intention to race anyway, regardless of M. Bochet's
orders, whereupon he warned them that half a squadron of

the 23rd Hussars and two cannon would be placed in the middle of the road at the start, with instructions to shoot anyone who tried to defy his ban. Determined to race, the ACF neatly circumnavigated the officious Bochet by switching the start from Paris to Villiers, which was outside his jurisdiction. The drivers proceeded to tow their cars to Villiers behind horses or transport them there by train, leaving the frustrated Bochet (and his army) to retreat to his office with his tail firmly between his legs.

At 8.30 the following morning Fernand Charron in a Panhard et Levassor was first away, followed by the rest of the 48-strong field at 30-second intervals. Charron's vehicle, one of the first racing cars to be fitted with a steering wheel instead of a tiller, maintained a strong pace to lead from Gilles Hourgières until a seized engine delayed Hourgières by as long as 15 hours and allowed Léonce Girardot's Panhard to move up to second. At the end of the first day 183 miles (295km) had been covered and Charron led Girardot by 12min 44sec. The 30 vehicles still remaining set off the following morning for Nijmegen but although Hourgières was the fastest on the road, he was unable to make up all the time he had lost back in France. On the third day, the competitors reached Amsterdam, by which time Charron's place at the head of affairs had been usurped by François Giraud in a Bollée, who led by three and a half minutes at the Dutch capital.

Following a day's rest in Amsterdam, the cars began the homeward journey, which soon developed into a battle between Charron and Girardot with Giraud close behind in third. After day five Charron was in the lead but he dropped back the following day, at the end of which Girardot led by an impressive nine minutes. Meanwhile Giraud had lost ground by overturning, although he managed to right the Bollée and reach Verdun in second place. Just when everything was set for a thrilling finish, M. Bochet reared his ugly head again, declaring that any driver whose car had not passed his original inspection would be arrested on arrival in Paris. Since this would have meant most of the entrants ending up in prison, the ACF outfoxed Bochet once more by moving the finish to Montgeron, just outside Paris, and therefore tantalisingly out of the policeman's clutches.

On the seventh and final day, Charron overtook both Giraud and Girardot by dint of suffering fewer punctures and arrived at Montgeron the winner, having covered the 889 miles (1,431km) in 33hr 4min 34sec at an average speed of 27mph (43.4km/h). Girardot finished second, just ahead of Giraud, to complete the anticipated French one-two-three.

In the meantime vast crowds had gathered at Versailles, where it had originally been intended that the race would finish. Cheated of their entertainment, they begged the organisers to send the winning cars forward from Montgeron. So Charron and Girardot drove on to Versailles, where they were mobbed by well-wishers. M. Bochet was poised to pounce but concluded that to arrest France's newest national heroes might provoke a riot. For once in his career, he reasoned that discretion was the better part of valour.

CHARRON IN REVERSE
TOUR DE FRANCE, 16 JULY 1899

Buoyed by the success of its enterprising racing calendar, the Automobile Club de France began preparations for the longest motor race in the world to date – a 1,423 mile (2,290km) circuit of France to be spread over nine days. The schedule was as follows:

Day 1 – Paris to Nancy (180 miles/290km)
Day 2 – Nancy to Aix-les-Bains (274 miles/441km)
Day 3 – Rest day
Day 4 – Aix-les-Bains to Vichy (238 miles/383km)
Day 5 – Rest day
Day 6 – Vichy to Périgueux (186 miles/299km)
Day 7 – Périgueux to Nantes (210 miles/338km)
Day 8 – Nantes to Cabourg (216 miles/348km)
Day 9 – Cabourg to Paris (119 miles/192km)

Sponsorship by *Le Matin* had attracted 48 starters – 19 cars, 25 motorcycles, and four lighter vehicles or voiturettes. The favourites were the French trio of Fernand Charron, René de Knyff and Léonce Girardot, whose Panhards had finished first, second and third in the Paris to Bordeaux race two months earlier. The start took place on a Sunday morning at the foot of a long hill just outside the Parisian suburban town of Champigny. One absentee was the Panhard driven by Comte Berthier de Savigny who, on his way to the start, tried to avoid a pedestrian in the centre of Paris, but went up on the pavement and knocked down a lamp-post. While the Comte was unharmed, the car was wrecked. Charron was first away at 8a.m., followed by Girardot 30 seconds later, the remainder of the field following at similar intervals. Last away was the Vallée car driven by Flash, a pseudonym for Dr E. Lewhess. It was expected to create an impression and it certainly did, although not quite in the way its driver had envisaged. For it was unable even to climb the first hill. It eventually reached the summit after ten long minutes but only because the mechanic got out and pushed. As if this ignominious start was not enough to have the good doctor reaching for his pills, a tyre then burst. With no spare on board, Lewhess had to catch a cab back to Paris to fetch a new one. Not surprisingly, he decided to retire shortly afterwards.

There were numerous hazards en route. Several drivers ended up in ditches trying to avoid spectators or wagons, while dogs were a constant menace, packs of them chasing the drivers through every village. The route was also littered with level crossings which damaged the wheels and suspensions, leading to further retirements. An added obstacle was that, on approaching Nancy at the end of the first day, the drivers discovered that a steep hill was not fit for vehicles, requiring them to seek an alternative way into the town. De Knyff led the field after that first stage, but Charron had forged ahead by Aix-les-Bains. The much-fancied Girardot suffered a setback when he broke a wheel but, resourceful as ever, he managed to borrow a replacement from a farmer's cart. It is not known whether he ever actually returned the wheel to the farmer. And Camille Jenatzy ended up in a ditch after smashing a wheel. He was able to continue after repairing the damage but had lost precious time.

At the outset of day four, de Knyff lost 30 minutes repairing the springs on his car and more time ebbed away when he stopped to help one of the motorcyclists, Williams, who had come off his machine. Nobly, de Knyff drove the injured rider to St Etienne, where Williams suddenly came to his senses and refused to let de Knyff help him further in case the delay cost him the race. Remarkably, de Knyff was able to make up the ground and finished the day five minutes ahead of Charron. Less fortunate was a M. Degrais, whose motorised tricycle skidded out of control after a chicken had got caught between the front wheel and the mudguard ...

Following the second rest day, there were 30 competitors still going at the start of day six. A minor – but time-consuming – accident to Charron put de Knyff 35 minutes ahead at Périgueux, by which time the field had been thinned to 23. De Knyff was still ahead at Nantes, and his victory was sealed on the next stage to Cabourg when Charron's forward transmission gear broke near Le Mans. Unable to go forward, Charron refused to admit defeat, turned the car round and drove the 25 miles (40.2km) to Alençon in reverse! Alas, the prospect of reversing all the way to Paris proved too daunting and he was forced to retire.

De Knyff was never troubled after that and went on to win the first prize of £240 by five hours from Girardot, with Comte Gaston de Chasseloup-Laubat third in another Panhard. De Knyff 's average speed was 30⅕mph (48.6km/h), and there were 20 finishers – ten cars, eight motorcycles and two voiturettes.

THE HOUND FROM HELL
GORDON BENNETT TROPHY,
14 JUNE 1900

Motor racing in France had received a temporary setback when Mme Bos, wife of a prominent French politician, suffered a broken leg after being hit by a car while watching a race from Paris to Roubaix. Every competitor in that race was immediately arrested on criminal charges and the future of the sport appeared in jeopardy. But any mutterings of discontent were quickly forgotten as Mme Bos regained the use of her leg and the French motor industry exercised its considerable influence. The French became the envy of the world, their escapades on the road reaching the ears of American newspaper magnate Gordon Bennett, publisher of the *New York Herald*, and the man hitherto best known for having sent Stanley off to find Livingstone. Bennett heard about a challenge issued by Fernand Charron to American motoring pioneer Alexander Winton and, in 1899, eager to end the French monopoly of motor racing and to encourage manufacturers in other countries – especially the United States – he proposed an international event bearing his own name. Ironically, the first Gordon Bennett Trophy race in 1900 was won by a Frenchman!

The race became a mainstay of the European motor racing scene at the turn of the century. It was a competition between teams of no more than three cars from each participating country, the winning nation having to organise the following year's event, rather like the Eurovision Song

Contest, although it has to be said that was where the similarity ended. When Englishman Selwyn Edge won the 1902 event in a Napier – largely by being the only finisher – this caused some embarrassment since motor racing was illegal on English roads. The difficulty was resolved by staging the 1903 Gordon Bennett race at the Athy circuit in Ireland. The Gordon Bennett races were also significant in being the first in which national racing colours were used. For 1900, France carried blue, Germany white, Belgium yellow, and the United States red.

That inaugural competition was held on French soil between Paris and Lyons, a journey of 353 miles (568km). The French selected Panhard as their official team, much to the disgust of Mors who decided to put forward its own entrant to prove that it was the equal of the powerful Panhards. So in addition to Fernand Charron, René de Knyff and Léonce Girardot in Panhards, 'Levegh' (the pseudonym of Pierre Velghe) drove a supposedly non-competing Mors. The overseas challenge was to be represented by Camille Jenatzy in a Bolide for Belgium; Eugen Benz in a Benz for Germany; and Alexander Winton and Anthony Riker in Wintons for the United States, the first American cars to compete in Europe. The Benz, however, withdrew because of tyre problems and Riker's Winton was not ready in time, leaving just five cars plus the rogue Mors.

To the embarrassment of the French, it was Levegh who set the early pace, soon building up a lead of half an hour over the three Panhards, followed by Jenatzy, with Winton a distant last. Then each car began to fall victim to problems of varying severity. De Knyff, Jenatzy and Winton all retired, Levegh was beset with mechanical difficulties, and Girardot got lost near Orléans! This left Charron in the lead even though he had bent the Panhard's rear axle driving over a gutter, as a result of which his faithful mechanic, Henri Fournier, had to trickle oil continuously on to the chains to keep the car going.

The saying about it never being over until the fat lady sings was never more true than in those early days of motor racing. Nobody could take victory for granted. However, the fat lady was definitely clearing her throat when, just 10 miles (16.1km) from the finish in Lyons, Charron's Panhard, powering downhill at 60mph (96.6km/h), was suddenly charged by a large dog. The animal went under the front wheels and finished up jammed in the steering, sending the car veering across a field before skidding back on to the road. There, Fournier calmly removed the dead dog before restarting the engine. But the collision had broken the water pump from its mounting, so as well as keeping a steady supply of oil on the chains, Fournier also had to hold the drive against the flywheel in order to keep the water circulating. He certainly had his hands full over those last 10 miles.

Eventually Charron struggled through to Lyons, winning from the unclassified Levegh and the geographically challenged Girardot. Panhard's blushes were spared, but only temporarily. For the following month Mors and Levegh gained their revenge by emphatically defeating their great rivals in the Paris-Toulouse race.

The Gordon Bennett Trophy remained a fixture until 1905 before being superseded by the French Grand Prix.

FUELLED BY ALCOHOL
CIRCUIT DU NORD, 15 MAY 1902

Around the turn of the century a series of rallies and races took place in France which were designed to promote alcohol as a fuel. The idea, by no means a new one, was born out of economic necessity. With few domestic oil reserves, France was eager to encourage the development of a fuel which could be readily distilled from domestic farm products. The French Ministry of Agriculture was certain that, when tested, alcohol would prove to be a viable – as well as cheaper – alternative to petrol.

Accordingly, in 1899 four alcohol-fuelled cars raced from Paris to Chantilly. The fact that only one completed the distance – and slowly – might have deterred some politicians from persevering with the experiment but within two years an assortment of 50 vehicles, ranging from lightweight quadricycles to heavy trucks, took part in a 167 mile (269km) run from Paris to Roubaix, an event sponsored by the Automobile Club of Paris. Fuels varied from pure alcohol to a mix of 50 per cent alcohol and 50 per cent petrol. Most drivers stated categorically that they preferred the 50-50 blend. Given the choice, they would undoubtedly have chosen pure petrol.

Undaunted, Minister of Agriculture Jean Dupuy organised his most ambitious project to date, the 537 mile (864km) Circuit du Nord, or the 'Alcohol Race' as it became known. The race was run in two heats – the first from Champigny to

Arras on day one; the second from Arras to St Germain (via Boulogne and Dieppe) on day two. A strict condition of the race was that all competitors used only fuel of pure alcohol – no mixers. However, enforcing this regulation proved well nigh impossible once the cars were out in the country and many drivers are believed to have used as little alcohol fuel as possible because it gave their vehicles reduced power. Instead they would sneak in supplies of petrol and hope to fool the scrutineers. Reports were rife of strange odours coming from behind certain cars ... A total of 85 had put their names down for the race but at the roll-call there were 20 absentees, among them Henri Fournier, winner of the Paris-Bordeaux and Paris-Berlin events of 1901. The competitors were split into three categories – heavy cars, light cars and voiturettes. The first man was away at 4a.m. sharp, the remainder following at respectful three-minute intervals. The first to reach Arras – and in the fastest time of 4hr 48min 5sec – was Frenchman Maurice Farman in a Panhard. The second arrival was fellow countryman Marcellin Javott in a Darracq. They were met by the enthusiastic M. Dupuy, who had travelled by special train to greet the victors and proceeded to deliver an optimistic speech on the virtues of alcohol which, he claimed, had proved its capacity to rival petrol. Little did he know of the skulduggery that was afoot.

The next day Farman left Arras at 4a.m. and reached St Germain at 1p.m., thereby winning the second heat as well. He was followed 58 minutes later by Englishman Charles Jarrott in another Panhard. When the results of the two heats were added together, Farman was declared the winner of the heavy car section at an average speed of 44⅕mph (72.1km/h), with Jarrott second. Javott's Darracq won the light car group at a speed of 41⅓mph (66.3km/h) and M. Grus's Renault was the quickest voiturette at 33⅔mph (54.7km/h).

The speeds – albeit enhanced by petrol – stood up reasonably well, and M. Dupuy remained convinced that alcohol fuel was the way forward. History would prove him wrong.

JARROTT'S RUNNING REPAIRS

PARIS TO VIENNA, 26 JUNE 1902

At the height of Europe's inter-city races, 148 competitors set off from Paris to Vienna in an event run concurrently with the annual Gordon Bennett race. The duality not only contributed to the excessive number of starters but also created a line-up of all shapes and sizes, from tiny Renaults to the more powerful but occasionally sluggish Panhards, Mors and Mercedes. The field included a number of wealthy amateurs, among them the colourful Count Eliot Zborowski in a Mercedes, the American driver William K. Vanderbilt in a Mors and another American, George Heath, in a Panhard.

Once the cars were away from Paris, hundreds of spectators rushed to board a special train for Belfort to witness the end of the first stage. Near Nangis the railway ran alongside the road and startled passengers watched as Henri Fournier's car sped past them at a speed approaching 80mph (129km/h). Fournier paid the price shortly afterwards when his car suffered a broken gear shaft. Well down the field in eighteenth at the conclusion of that first section was Frenchman Marcel Renault in a little 16hp car made by Renault Frères, the company he had founded with his brother Louis. Although he couldn't hope to match the bigger cars on the fast stretches, Renault came into his own on the twisty mountainous sections, notably on the third day when the field tackled the 5,912 foot Arlberg peak in western Austria. The descent from the mountain was extremely dangerous because car brakes had never previously been subjected to such a rigorous test, but Renault coped admirably and made up so much ground through Switzerland and Austria that he held a clear lead by the time he reached Vienna on 29 June after four days of hard driving. Then right at the death he nearly threw it away. The finish was in a trotting track on the outskirts of the city, but on entering the stadium, Renault drove round the track the wrong way. The race organisers insisted that he leave the stadium and re-enter in the proper manner – a detour which cost him 15 minutes and meant that his margin of victory over Count Zborowski was much smaller than it would otherwise have been. Six other Renaults made it to the finish, including brother Louis despite his car being hit by the Mercedes of Baron de Caters while waiting to check in at the Salzburg control. The collision left the Renault with several broken spokes in one of the front wheels. With no spare wheel, Louis' intrepid mechanic found some wood and used a sharp knife to create makeshift spokes strong enough to take the car through Austria to the finish.

However, the misfortunes of the Renault brothers were nothing compared to the adventures experienced by Charles Jarrott at the wheel of a 13.72-litre Panhard. On the second day of the race the car's wooden chassis collapsed just short of the overnight stop at Bregenz in Austria. Jarrott and his mechanic, George Du Cros, felt that if they could somehow strengthen the frame, it might carry them through the next stage to Salzburg at the very least. They managed to acquire a drill and some bolts but attempts to find four long pieces of wood proved fruitless, until inspiration came just as Jarrott was preparing to settle down for the night at their hotel. He later wrote: 'I was just getting into bed and had turned to put out the light, when my eye fell upon a stand used for carrying a tray, and in a second I perceived that the four legs of that stand were exactly what I wanted.'

Conveniently reasoning that it was too late at night to ask the hotel manager whether he would be interested in selling them the stand, they set about dismantling it anyway and drilled four holes in each length of wood so that in the morning they could bolt the pieces on each side of the broken chassis frame. The wood being extremely resilient, Du Cros had the bright idea of drilling against the wall. 'He was delightfully successful,' recorded Jarrott, 'but the trouble was that he drove it through too far, and brought down half the plaster. And then, in endeavouring to show how easy it was on another portion of the wall, he succeeded in bringing that down also.' At that juncture Jarrott managed to drill a hole through his arm instead of the wood and for the next half-hour the pair had to rip up bed linen for bandages. 'There was nothing in the room we did not utilise for something or other,' said Jarrott. 'I hate to think what must have been the expression on the proprietor's face when he discovered what had taken place.'

The following morning they evaded detection by creeping out of the hotel at first light and were on the road by seven o'clock, reaching Salzburg just in time to scotch a rumour (which *The Times* correspondent was in the act of cabling to London) that they had been killed in a crash. The makeshift chassis did its job, although at one point on the final stage Du Cros had to lie full length along the bonnet with a towel wrapped around the pipe to prevent water from leaking from the radiator. But then, no more than 3 miles (4.8km) from Vienna, the distorted chassis frame caused the gearbox to break and lumps of machinery fell into the road. The indefatigable Jarrott commandeered a bicycle and pedalled off to get help. He returned to find Du Cros being towed towards the finish behind a horse-drawn cab. This ignominy was too much for Jarrott to take and he promptly slashed the tow rope and jumped behind the wheel. As the car rumbled away, belching smoke and flame, the exhaust box fell off. The gearless monster lurched uncontrollably across the finish line, at which point it finally expired. It wouldn't move another yard, but Jarrott and Du Cros were unconcerned. Against all the odds, they had completed the Paris to Vienna motor race.

THE RACE TO DEATH
PARIS TO MADRID, 24 MAY 1903

When road racing was first introduced to Europe less than a decade earlier, the sedate speeds posed relatively little threat to spectators or participants. But the technological advances which had been made in the motor industry in the intervening years had enabled cars to achieve speeds in excess of 90mph (145km/h). Clearly this represented a considerable hazard on public roads, especially to a public which was still not fully accustomed to the motor car. The death of a boy spectator during the 1901 Paris-Berlin race had resulted in the French government banning all road racing in France, but when the 1902 Paris-Vienna marathon passed off without any fatalities, the authorities bowed to pressure to allow racing to resume on public thoroughfares. In doing so, they gave the green light to a contest which would be known thereafter as the 'race to death'. The Auto Club de France came up with the idea of a three-day race from Paris to Madrid – a distance of 872 miles (1,403km), much of it over roads which had barely seen a motor car. The first day was to take the drivers 342 miles (550km) through Chartres, Tours, Poitiers and Angoulême to Bordeaux. The second and third days were to be spent negotiating the treacherous tracks across the Guadarrama mountains near Madrid. This was reckoned to be the most difficult section of the route, but in the event, none of the drivers got that far.

King Alfonso of Spain raised no objections to the proposed race and when the French government also consented, planning began in earnest for what was expected to be a major spectacle for both countries. Indeed no fewer than three million spectators lined the route between Paris and Bordeaux. The starters – 275 in all – were divided into four groups. There were 112 in the heavy car group (including 1.5-litre Panhards and 12.5-litre Mercedes); 64 light cars; 40 voiturettes (the section for vehicles under 1.5 litres); and 59 motorcycles. To reduce weight, most of the cars were stripped down to the bare minimum with the result that the drivers sat on nothing more comfortable than a wooden plank. The entrants gathered at Versailles on Sunday 24 May for a 3.45a.m. start, which, even by the standards of those days, was unreasonably early. First to go was Charles Jarrott in a De Dietrich, the remainder following at one-minute intervals. So by the time the final car was away, the leaders were 135 miles (217km) off down the road.

The Renault brothers were again to the fore, Marcel having a starting number of 39 and Louis being third away. When the two cars in front of Louis fell back, he had the benefit of a clear road ahead from Rambouillet to Bordeaux while those behind had to battle through clouds of dust. Louis Renault duly reached Bordeaux at 12.15p.m. after some eight and a half hours on the road, having averaged over 62mph (99.8km/h). He was followed 16 minutes later by Jarrott, but behind him there was carnage. Marcel Renault had worked his way up to third when, travelling at speed between Poitiers and Angoulême, he put two wheels in a ditch while trying to overtake a slower car. Marcel's car overturned and he was killed. On the outskirts of Bordeaux, Lorraine Barrow's De Dietrich swerved off the road in trying to avoid a dog. The car smashed into a tree, killing Barrow's companion Pierre Rodez. Stray spectators were as great a danger as dogs. At one point a child ran into the road in front of a Brouhot driven by M. Touran. In taking evasive action, the unfortunate Touran careered into a crowd of onlookers. His own passenger, one spectator and the errant child were all killed. In another horrific smash, Leslie Porter's Wolseley veered out of control on the approach to a level crossing, ploughed into a house and caught fire. His riding mechanic, Nixon, was thrown to his death.

The exact figures vary, but following around nine deaths and countless injuries, the French Prime Minister, Emile Combes, ordered the race to be stopped at Bordeaux. It was all too apparent that spectators had no regard for their own safety and that today's motor cars were simply too fast for racing on public highways. The authorities suddenly became so jumpy that, having called a halt to proceedings, they would not even permit the cars to be driven under their own power to Bordeaux railway station in readiness for the return trip to Paris. Instead each car had to be towed to the station by horse. The inevitable backlash to the tragedy followed, both French and Spanish governments issuing edicts banning all further racing. Paris to Madrid would go down in history as the last of the great city-to-city races.

Amid the rows and recriminations, the outcome of the curtailed race was almost incidental. Yet there were some heroic performances, including that of Madame Camille du Gast in a 5.7-litre De Dietrich. An accomplished and versatile sportswoman, she had attained the lofty heights of fifth place by the town of Châtellerault, north of Poitiers, before dropping back to forty-fifth after stopping to help a fellow competitor who had been involved in an accident. In the end, first place was awarded to Fernand Gabriel who, having started a lowly eighty-second, reached Bordeaux in his 12-litre Mors in third place, just 40 minutes behind Charles Jarrott. His average speed of 65⅓mph (105km/h) put him ahead of Louis Renault, Joseph Salleron in a Mors and Jarrott. But few people, least of all Louis Renault who had just lost his brother, felt much like celebrating.

JOURNEY INTO THE UNKNOWN

PEKING TO PARIS, 10 JUNE 1907

In the aftermath of the Paris-Madrid débâcle, motor racing in France kept a low profile for a couple of years. But the staging of the first French Grand Prix in 1906 once again whetted the appetite of the pioneer motorists, and thoughts turned to an epic test of endurance rather than one of pure speed. On 31 January 1907 the celebrated French newspaper *Le Matin* carried the following headline on its front page: 'PARIS-PEKING AUTOMOBILE: A Stupendous Challenge.' The article dismissed circuit races such as the Grand Prix and accused organisers of motor races of failing to realise the car's full potential. 'The whole *raison d'être* of cars is that they make possible the most ambitious and unpremeditated trips to far horizons. For this reason the general public fails to see the logic of making motor cars chase their tails in tight circles ... What needs to be proved today is that as a man has a car he can do anything and go anywhere.' Then came the killer question: 'Is there anyone who will undertake to travel this summer from Paris to Peking by automobile?'

The first to respond was the Count de Dion, doyen of the French motor industry, who replied in heroic terms: 'It is my belief that if a motor car can get through, the De Dion-Bouton will get through. I take up this challenge here and now.' The challenge also captured the imagination of Prince Scipione Borghese, an Italian nobleman, who wasted no time in ordering a car from the Itala factory in Turin. By the end of the first week in February as many as ten works teams were believed to have expressed serious interest in the great adventure. The organisers then decided to reverse the route so that the race started in Peking and finished in Paris. This would not only avoid the beginning of the rainy season in China, where the 'roads' were nothing more than dirt tracks, but would also provide *Le Matin* with the glorious spectacle of a Parisian climax.

Although 25 teams would eventually consider taking part, many were scared away by the entry fee of 2,200 francs and, as the day drew nearer, by the sheer enormity of the task. In the end the starting line-up was just five. Prince Borghese, who appeared singularly undaunted by the trans-continental trek, was very much the race favourite in his four-cylinder, 7.4-litre Itala in which he was joined by mechanic Ettore Guizzardi and Milan journalist Luigi Barzini, whose account of the race would grace the pages of, among other publications, *The Daily Telegraph*. Borghese's rivals were former jockey and stunt motorcyclist Charles Godard, driving a four-cylinder Dutch Spyker with Jean du Taillis as his passenger; Georges Cormier and passenger Edgardo Longini in a two-cylinder De Dion-Bouton; Victor Collignon with mechanic Jean Bizac in an identical De Dion-Bouton; and last, and certainly least, Auguste Pons and mechanic Octave Foucault in an alarmingly lightweight one-cylinder Contal tri-car, a vehicle so small that it had no room for serious rations or bedding – something of a handicap when planning to spend the next three months travelling across the wilds of Mongolia and Siberia. From Peking, the route was to take them north-west to Mongolia, across the barren Gobi desert, over the uncharted plains of Siberia and eastern Russia to Moscow, and then, via more recognisable roads, to Warsaw, Berlin and Paris. The total race distance was some 10,000 miles (16,093km). Even getting to Peking in the first place was an ordeal, Borghese being obliged to cross Asia on horse, camel and foot. It was scarcely the ideal preparation, but seemed to have no adverse effect on the redoubtable Italian.

It was with a degree of unease that the Chinese authorities observed the start in their capital at 8a.m. on 10 June. The State Council of the Celestial Chinese Empire feared that these 'fuel chariots' were using the race as a cover for surveying routes by which the West could invade China at some future date. The Council were also concerned that these strange machines might exert a disturbing influence on the Chinese people and declared that they wanted the cars out of Peking as quickly as possible in the belief that 'they would cause an upheaval in the popular mind and spread everywhere the fatal germs of western corruption'. Given the unpredictable nature of the route through China, the quintet of drivers agreed to stay in convoy until they reached Irkutsk in Russia, after which the race could begin in earnest. It was an admirable notion, but one which foundered almost immediately when, barely a quarter of a mile (0.4km) out of Peking, Collignon and Pons both succeeded in getting lost. Godard fared little better. Unable to read a map, he had only the vaguest idea of geography. His Spyker was decorated in vertical stripes of red, white and blue and along the body were painted the words SIBERIA, RUSSIA, GERMANY. This was supposedly to inform passers-by of the route, but there was also the suggestion that it served to remind Godard which way to go. The hopelessly inadequate Contal was struggling so badly on the uneven Chinese roads that Pons decided to retrace his steps and complete the first leg to Nankow by train. The other four pressed on, but took seven days to cover the initial 200 miles (322km), constantly being delayed by having to be manhandled over ancient bridges on the Peking plain. Teams of coolies with mules had to drag the cars through the Nankow Gorge and over the mountains towards the Great Wall after first stripping the bodywork to a bare minimum and removing all provisions on board. The Chinese routes – constructed from broken stones and huge boulders – were frequently impassable, necessitating the use of a pick-axe to smash a path for the cars. As a result of the appalling Chinese road surfaces, the cars could not run unaided until the Mongolian plateau had been reached.

It was in the Gobi desert that the Contal finally gave up the ghost. Once again Pons had become lost and had fallen way behind the others. Tired of having to carry his supplies and of repeatedly having to go back and search for him, the remaining four decided not to bother this time. The Contal ran out of fuel and was eliminated from the race.

The abysmal lack of preparation by the Contal team was in stark contrast to Borghese's crew. In advance they had sent camel caravans out into the desert to lay down supplies of fuel, tyres and provisions at strategic points. For the best part of 800 miles (1,287km) across the Gobi the cars doggedly followed telegraph wires until, in the words of Barzini, 'they seemed to be taking a wrong direction for our purpose'. Then the Itala would veer off into the wilderness 'for hours and hours, with no guide except our common sense'. The extra power of the Itala gave it a considerable advantage in terms of speed but its weight proved a handicap when crossing Mongolian marshland. Between Urga and Kiakhta the car suddenly sank in a bog. Passing tribesmen took one look at the sinking car and continued on their way but, by a stroke of good fortune, a team of Mongolian horsemen appeared on the scene. They wedged planks under the wheels and got their oxen to pull but this had no effect until someone had the bright idea of starting the engine. Barzini recalled: 'At the sudden noise, the four terrified beasts pulled desperately, and suddenly the car came out of its furrow with one bound.' Following this close shave, Borghese and his crew carefully reconnoitred any suspect ground before driving over it. Eventually they reached the River Iro, where they again required the services of local oxen to haul the car through waist-high water. They were a day ahead of the rest of the field by the time they reached the Russian border, 'our faces literally black with dust, and over our clothes a thick crust of the different kinds of mud with which we had come in intimate contact all along our way'.

The 6,000 mile (9,656km) journey across Siberia and Russia was distinctly uncomfortable for Borghese and his men, travelling in an open car in what was often torrential rain. Borghese's only protection was the pith helmet which he wore for much of the race. To make matters worse, following the construction of the Trans-Siberian Railway, much of the Siberian highway system was in a state of chronic disrepair, deteriorating into a series of bumpy tracks and treacherous bogs. At Lake Baikal, the road and bridges were impassable, so Borghese obtained permission to drive on the railway track! When forced to make a hasty detour by road because of an approaching train, the Itala fell foul of a rickety wooden bridge which collapsed under the car's weight, almost crushing Borghese, Barzini and Ettore. The car was eventually winched to safety from the ravine by a gang of Siberian railway workers and returned to the relative security of the railway track, only to endure another near miss seconds later when surprised by a freight train. Later in the Ural mountains a rear wheel collapsed on the Itala, its wooden spokes weakened by the muddy roads. A local wagon-builder – the only one for hundreds of miles – made an effective replacement. Behind, the other crews hitched their cars to half-wild horses in order to ford Siberian rivers and carried out emergency repairs with rashers of raw bacon. The unscrupulous Godard reportedly resorted to theft so as to stay in the race.

Prince Borghese reached Moscow while the other competitors were still battling through Siberia. With a lead of 18 days, he could even afford to take a lengthy detour up to St Petersburg before heading down triumphantly through Germany, Belgium and northern France. Despite losing additional time on social engagements, the prince increased his lead through Europe, entering the French capital on 10 August flanked by well-wishers as well as three brand new Italas which had been sent out to greet him by the firm's Paris agent. Covering 10,000 miles in 60 days across some of the world's most inhospitable terrain was, after all, a pretty good advertisement for the car's sturdiness and reliability. Pulling up in front of the offices of *Le Matin*, Borghese explained the secret of his success to reporters: 'We never thought of the final goal, never admitted that our end was Paris. Every day when we awoke we concentrated on nothing but getting the day's stage done well.' He added: 'Such a journey requires more patience than daring.'

It was a further 20 days before the Spyker and the two De Dions arrived together in Paris. Godard had been arrested in Germany on the orders of *Le Matin*, who wanted the two French cars to beat him, but had managed to talk his way out of trouble and resume his place behind the wheel.

Following its remarkable victory, the Itala was in great demand and, along with the two De Dions, was shown in London at the 1908 Olympia Motor Show. However, the car met an untimely end when, en route to being shipped to New York for another exhibition, it rolled into the dockside water at Genoa. The car was eventually salvaged but was badly damaged. The Itala thus went down in history as being the only car to survive a 10,000 mile race but not the subsequent exhibition.

THE RACE AROUND THE WORLD

NEW YORK TO PARIS, 12 FEBRUARY 1908

A matter of weeks after the finish of the Peking to Paris race, *Le Matin* joined forces with the *New York Times* to announce another motoring marathon, one which would encircle the globe from New York to Paris. To put it mildly, the planned route was ambitious, incorporating a winter overland journey through western Canada and Alaska, followed by a trip across the ice of the Bering Straits to Russia! *The Motor* dismissed the whole idea as 'mad-brained'. Not surprisingly, one or two revisions had to be made once the event was under way.

Seven cars were due to start, but an Itala was withdrawn at the last minute when it emerged that the race organisers were going to handicap its time by the small matter of a week, presumably on account of the company's success in the Peking-Paris jaunt. As it was, six vehicles lined up outside the *New York Times* offices in Times Square. There were French cars – a Motobloc (driven by Peking-Paris survivor Charles Godard), a De Dion-Bouton and a Sizaire-Naudin; an Italian Züst, driven by Antonio Scarfoglio, poet, writer and son of a Naples newspaper publisher; the American Thomas Flyer, piloted by George Schuster; and a German Protos, entered in the name of the Kaiser and driven by Lt Hans Koeppen of the 15th Prussian infantry. The Kaiser had sent a special greeting to the German team. A crowd of over 250,000 New Yorkers watched the cars set off amid flying champagne corks and much waving of national flags. In readiness for the gruelling journey which lay ahead, each vehicle carried spare parts, shovels, sails, skis, food and, just in case, firearms.

If the competitors were expecting a comparatively trouble-free ride until they hit Alaska, they were sorely mistaken. For the worst weather in the whole race was reserved for New York State. Thick snow and mud rendered roads impassable, prompting the unscrupulous Godard to put the Motobloc on a train, a deed which resulted in his instant disqualification. The Sizaire-Naudin also dropped out shortly afterwards with a broken back axle. The remaining four ploughed west but, after three weeks of motoring, they had only got as far as Chicago. The intention had been to ship the cars to Alaska from Seattle on 10 March but the snow had completely disrupted the timetable. With its American factory able to provide the best service for this section of the race, the Thomas Flyer led the way across the Midwest. When the car became stuck in deep mud in Nebraska, local farmers dug it out. Worse was to follow in Wyoming, when the three-man crew found the route blocked by snow and were obliged to drive along 45 miles (72.4km) of railroad track from Carter to Evanston. This would subsequently be used in evidence against them.

The Thomas arrived in San Francisco on 24 March and four days later Schuster set sail for Alaska. Once there, it quickly became apparent that the Arctic crossing was a non-starter and so he began to retrace his steps, only to discover that the Protos, having been bogged down in the Wyoming mud, had travelled from Ogden, Utah, by train to Seattle and caught a ship to Russia. Meanwhile the De Dion and the Züst had boarded a boat to Japan. In a panic, *Le Matin* suddenly announced that the great slog across America had been to no avail since the race was now going to be restarted from Vladivostok! As a concession to the efforts of the Thomas crew in actually reaching Alaska, it was granted a 22-day bonus which allowed it to catch up with the others. Conversely, the Protos was penalised for 30 days for travelling by train. The entire event was degenerating into a shambles, attracting scorn from motoring publications. *The Autocar* – as the magazine was known in those days – commented: 'Seeing that the organisers are endeavouring to simplify the race as much as possible, it may be suggested whether, after all, it would not have been more satisfactory to ship the cars from New York to Le Havre, and then proceed by road to Paris.'

The crossing to Japan passed without incident and when Schuster arrived at the Maibara Inn in a rural region of the country, it was recorded as being the first time that a motor car had ever been seen there. After negotiating the dirt tracks of Japan, the three cars were loaded on to another ship bound for Vladivostok where they met up with the Protos. However, in protest at the rail journeys made by both the Thomas and the Protos, the De Dion was withdrawn on the orders of the Count himself, leaving just three cars to set off from Vladivostok at the restart on 22 May.

The Thomas again set the pace, albeit at a sloth-like 10 miles (16.1km) per day as it struggled through the boggy conditions. Following the tracks of the Peking-Paris pioneers, it then took to the line of the Trans-Siberian Railway until the gearbox broke, allowing the Protos to seize the initiative. In the meantime the Züst crew were nearly drowned on what they thought was dry land, and on another occasion they improvised a new crankshaft bearing from a cough sweet tin, some mud, some pieces of wood, and a quantity of bullets. As the race entered Europe, *Le Matin* panicked again, this time at the prospect of a German car, the Protos, being the first to reach Paris. So the newspaper changed the rules, altering the Protos's finishing point to Berlin. The Züst was to proceed to Paris, as planned, while the Thomas Flyer was ordered to make its way back to New York via transatlantic shipping. Fortunately nobody paid any attention to *Le Matin*'s instructions and the Protos drove on to Paris, arriving there on the night of 30 July to what one observer described as an 'embarrassed silence'. Four days later, having covered 13,341 miles (21,470km) in 169 days, the Thomas car reached Paris to a triumphant welcome and an immediate declaration of victory. It was now that the fun really started, with all three cars claiming victory.

Schuster was certain that he was the winner because, despite finishing four days behind the Protos, he thought the German car had incurred a 30-day penalty. There was also the small matter of the Protos missing out Japan completely. The Germans responded by accusing the Americans of having themselves travelled by rail across Wyoming. Then there was the Züst team. They didn't arrive in Paris for another two months, having been delayed at Omsk where the crew were seized as spies when they tried to send a cable in Italian. On eventually reaching France, they immediately claimed victory as theirs, insisting that the other two had cheated.

When all the fuss had died down, the organisers confirmed the Thomas Flyer as the winner. The race provided a massive boost to the US motor industry with sales of the Thomas jumping by 27 per cent. George Schuster became a national celebrity. Fate was less kind to the Züst. With eerie echoes of the fate of the victorious Itala from the Peking-Paris event, this latest Italian model was taken to England after the race, only to be destroyed by fire at a railway station.

THE FIRING SQUAD
US GRAND PRIZE, 26 NOVEMBER 1908

Although the home of motor racing was Europe, the sport
had started to take off in the United States. However, the
hopes of attracting the leading European drivers had been
dealt a severe blow by the 1906 Vanderbilt Cup race at Long
Island, New York – an event marred by poor crowd control.
Many drivers had felt intimidated by spectators who had
broken through the wire netting barriers and swamped the
circuit. So the authorities decided to take no chances for
the Grand Prize of the Automobile Club of America, to be
run on Thanksgiving Day, 1908, at Savannah, Georgia, and
arranged for the track to be patrolled by armed soldiers and
policemen. These officers didn't quite operate a 'shoot to
kill' policy, but they were decidedly trigger-happy.

The 25 mile (40.2km) Savannah circuit wound its way
along roads lined with palm trees, and the race distance of
402 miles (647km) was relatively short for that time. There
were 20 entrants, including a strong European contingent
with three Fiats and three Italas from Italy, three Benz cars
from Germany and two Renaults from France. The Fiat
team consisted of Felice Nazzaro, Louis Wagner and Ralph
de Palma, a young Italian-born American driving in his first
big race. His riding mechanic was Pietro Bordino, who went
on to become the leading Italian driver of the early 1920s. In
addition there were six American drivers – Ralph Mulford,
Joe Seymour, Bob Burman, Willie Haupt, Len Zengle and

Hugh Harding – each at the wheel of an American car. The Fiats and Renaults appeared to have a major advantage when it came to tyre stops thanks to the introduction of detachable rims. When a car sustained a puncture, the old tyre usually had to be slashed off with a knife, then a new inner tube and outer casing had to be fitted using levers before finally being inflated. It was a laborious process which resulted in lengthy pit stops. But Fiat and Renault were now using detachable rims which could be unbolted and bolted back on complete, thereby reducing the time taken by around ten minutes.

Following an extensive ten days of practice, the race was due to start at 9a.m. but was postponed 45 minutes because of fog. As was the norm in those days, the cars were started at intervals (massed starts not being widely introduced until 1922) with the result calculated on time rather than finishing position on the track. When the cars got away, it was de Palma who took the lead, followed by Wagner, René Hanriot in a Benz and with the fancied Nazzaro back in sixth. De Palma retained his lead until the third lap when tyre trouble dropped him back to last place. This allowed Hanriot to take over at the head of the field, pursued by Hungarian driver Ferenc Szisz in a Renault, Wagner, Victor Hémery (Benz) and Nazzaro. All the while the militia men, rifles poised, were keeping a close watch on the spectators. Then suddenly for some inexplicable reason, one of the locals tried to drive a horse and buggy across the track at the height of the race. The soldiers fired on the driver in an instant. He got the message.

Hanriot maintained his advantage until lap eight, by which time Hémery had moved up to second. As Hanriot fell away, Hémery began to dispute the lead with Nazzaro and Wagner. On lap 11 Erle, who was in fourth place, was knocked unconscious when a tyre burst and his Benz careered along the course for a further quarter of a mile (0.4km) before overturning. Luckily he received only minor injuries and his mechanic escaped unhurt. Then came more drama when the police captain shot at Hanriot for what was described as an infringement of the regulations. Somehow the black flag seems a more civilised method of dealing with transgressions. Remarkably, Hanriot bore no ill feelings and later presented his gloves and goggles to the officer.

Starting the final lap, Nazzaro had a lead of nearly two minutes over Hémery who, in turn, was just two seconds ahead of Wagner. Hanriot, still running despite his scare, was 12 minutes back in fourth. But 15 miles (24.1km) from the finish Nazzaro lost a tyre and was relegated to third. Hémery crossed the line first but it was Wagner who, by virtue of a storming last lap, was declared the winner on corrected time – by 57 seconds after more than six hours of racing. Wagner and Hémery made it a French one-two with the Italian Nazzaro back in third.

Despite the over-zealous policing, the event was declared a resounding success. The drivers much preferred Savannah to Long Island and were delighted when the 1910 Grand Prize was switched from New York to Georgia. For that occasion, a new course was laid out using convict labour, the prisoners being rewarded with a special enclosure on race day. 'It will be grand,' enthused Hémery. 'Not even Europe has ever furnished a more perfectly patrolled course.' Then again, he hadn't been shot at in 1908.

DOGGED BY MISFORTUNE
FRENCH GRAND PRIX, 25 JUNE 1912

Following a three-year break, the world's oldest Grand Prix reappeared on the calendar with a two-day race at Dieppe over a distance of 956 miles (1,538km), making it the longest event of the century at that point. It was also the last race of the giant cars, many of which were almost as high as a man. Since the only entry specification was a minimum cockpit width of 175mm (6⅞in), an army of these monster machines was unleashed on the Dieppe circuit – 17-litre Lorraine-Dietrichs and 14-litre Fiats dwarfing the 7.6-litre Peugeots and especially the little Sunbeams which were competing in the 3-litre voiturette class for the Coupe de l'Auto. The latter was run in conjunction with the Grand Prix and attracted an entry of 33 cars. Despite a partial German boycott, there were 14 vehicles taking part in the Grand Prix (an Excelsior, three Fiats, four Lorraines, one Mathis, two Rolland-Pilains and three Peugeots), making a total of 47.

With size considered to be everything, the clear favourites were the Fiats and the Lorraines. Among the Fiat drivers were the American amateur David Bruce-Brown and fellow countryman Ralph de Palma, who was due a change of luck. The previous month he had looked a certain winner of the Indianapolis 500 until his engine failed with two laps remaining. De Palma and his mechanic, Rupert Jeffkins, bravely pushed the car towards the finish, only to be overtaken.

During the week prior to the race Dieppe was invaded by motor racing fans of all nationalities. The casino did excellent business and the authorities organised a series of boxing contests to entertain the visitors. Hotel accommodation was at a premium, rooms being let for four days only – two days preceding the Grand Prix and the two days of the race itself. So anyone wishing to stay for just two days had to pay for four. As a result of this blatant exploitation, many followers preferred to camp out around the circuit.

The cars were flagged away from 5.30a.m. at 30-second intervals in front of a packed grandstand even at such an early hour. Victor Rigal's Sunbeam was first away for the voiturettes and Victor Hémery in his huge Lorraine was the first Grand Prix car to start, at 5.33. Hémery was also the first to reappear at the end of the opening 47 mile (75.6km) lap at 6.12a.m., but the race leader was Bruce-Brown in the Fiat S74, who came round ten minutes later having taken 37min 18sec for the lap. Georges Boillot was second in a Peugeot with Hémery third and Jules Goux fourth in another Peugeot. Hémery suffered engine failure on the second lap and a lap later Goux dropped from third to forticth so that after five laps (quarter-distance for the race), Bruce-Brown led from Boillot and Louis Wagner's Fiat. The leading positions remained unaltered for the rest of the day and at the end of that ten-lap session, Bruce-Brown led Boillot by 2min 1sec with Wagner nearly half an hour back in third. A highly creditable fourth was Dario Resta in a little Sunbeam. A total of 19 cars were still going. Bruce-Brown's driving had been a revelation, particularly his smooth, fast cornering. Nowhere was this more evident than at the S bend near the railway bridge at Ancourt, where a bugler was stationed to give audible warning of each car as it approached. The Fiat cars had on the whole been very impressive, too, being described as 'running with gyroscopic steadiness as solidly as the proverbial rock'.

Their Achilles' heel, however, was pit stops. Although the new tarred road surfaces represented a vast improvement on the old dirt tracks, the Fiats were extremely hard on tyres and had to stop for regular wheel changes. The Italian company had made the mistake of persisting with fixed wooden wheels with detachable rims instead of the newly invented detachable wire wheels with knock-off hubs that were favoured by Peugeot. As a result Fiat pit stops were considerably longer than those of Peugeot. Fiat also lost valuable time refuelling by churn and funnel, whereas Peugeot used a more advanced pressure system. So despite the fact that the Fiats were markedly quicker on the road – as would be expected from their superior power – the delays caused by pit stops kept them within reach of their French rivals. Nevertheless Bruce-Brown, in his familiar woollen windsock hat, was in pole position and was confident of cementing a famous victory on the second day. The cars started the second day at the intervals and in the order in which they had finished the first ... minus René Hanriot's Lorraine which had mysteriously caught fire overnight. The race conditions had also changed during the hours of darkness, persistent rain having created a slippery surface which suited Boillot better than Bruce-Brown. Consequently the Frenchman steadily whittled away at the lead until after two laps on the second day (12 overall), Bruce-Brown's advantage was down to a mere 11 seconds. Bruce-Brown was still ahead when, out in the country, his car had the misfortune to collide with a stray dog, an impact which ruptured the fuel tank, causing it to leak. As he struggled to carry on, he was promptly disqualified for refuelling away from the pits. De Palma and Goux fell foul of the same rule.

Profiting from the hound's intervention, Boillot moved into first place and stayed there. His only worrying moment occurred on the penultimate lap when the Peugeot suffered a jammed gearbox. It took Boillot and riding mechanic

Charles Prévost 20 minutes to fix it and they set off again, but with only second and fourth gears. Fortunately Boillot's lead was such that he was able to coast home by 13 minutes from Wagner with Rigal third and Resta fourth. By finishing third, fourth and fifth overall, the Sunbeams easily won the Coupe de l'Auto. As for Bruce-Brown, he kept going to the finish despite his disqualification, but never again would a car of over 10-litres come so close to winning a classic road race. And later that year he was killed during practice for the US Grand Prize at Milwaukee.

CHAMPAGNE JULES
INDIANAPOLIS 500, 30 MAY 1913

The 2½ mile (4km) oval circuit at Indianapolis was laid down in 1909 at a cost of $250,000. The original surface was natural rock which had been steamrollered flat, but this proved too dangerous and so the circuit was paved with three million bricks, earning it the nickname of 'The Brickyard'. This surface remained until 1935 when, with the exception of the start/finish straight, the track was asphalted. The last of the brick paving disappeared in 1961 when the entire circuit, apart from a symbolic brick strip at the finish line, was asphalted. Until 1971, the 200 lap, 500 mile (805km) spectacular was raced on Memorial Day, the day each year on which the United States remembers its war dead, but that year it was moved to the last Sunday in May. The first '500' took place in 1911 and the following year Ralph Mulford completed the race down the field at a leisurely 56mph (90.1km/h) solely to qualify for starting money, even stopping for lunch on the way! In 1913 it was drink rather than food which would make the headlines.

The first two years of the '500' had been essentially an American preserve, but in 1913 there was a significant European challenge. Five foreign drivers ('swarthy skinned aliens' as the American press called them) took part and the line-up included eight foreign cars – two Peugeots, two Mercedes and three Isotta-Fraschinis and a Sunbeam. As the American cars were much smaller than their European counterparts, none of the monster machines were entered. Of the European contingent only Frenchman Jules Goux had any experience of a banked circuit like Indianapolis, having raced in the spring of that year at Brooklands where he had lapped at a highly impressive 109⅕mph (175.8km/h). For Indianapolis Goux was at the wheel of the same 7.4-litre Peugeot in which Georges Boillot had won the eventful 1912 French Grand Prix. It was to prove a good omen.

America's Robert Evans led for the first few laps in a Mason but the race soon settled down into a battle between the Peugeots of Goux and Paul Zuccarelli, American Bob Burman in a 7.2-litre Keeton, and Albert Guyot in the strongly fancied Sunbeam. Alas, Guyot did not enjoy one of his more auspicious drives. R.F. Crossman accompanied him as riding mechanic and some observers thought the Sunbeam might have fared better had the situations been reversed. For despite having to change just one tyre throughout the 500 miles, Guyot could only finish a disappointing fourth, never really threatening the leaders. Up front, Goux made numerous tyre stops and during each one he guzzled a quantity of the Frenchman's favourite tipple, champagne. In the course of the race, he downed no fewer than six bottles! Far from having an adverse effect on his driving, the alcohol intake spurred him on to greater heights and when Burman dropped out in the second 100 miles (161km), then Zuccarelli retired with carburettor trouble while lying second, Goux was left unchallenged in the lead. He went on to become the first European to win at Indianapolis (pocketing the prize money of £8,750), finishing well ahead of Spencer Wishart's 4.9-litre Mercer, which crossed the line on fire, and Charlie Merz's Stutz.

Goux's triumph saw him acclaimed as a national hero on his return to Paris. Over the ensuing years there was much debate as to whether or not the champagne story was apocryphal, but Goux himself subsequently confirmed that it was definitely champagne and not water that he had consumed during those pit stops. He added that it was the finest vintage, procured before the race with great difficulty by a Mr Kaufman of New York, Peugeot's representative in the United States.

ACROSS THE LINE
BACKWARDS
TARGA FLORIO, 23 NOVEMBER 1919

The brainchild of Count Vincenzo Florio, the Targa Florio was first run in Sicily in 1906. When the suggestion of staging a race on the mountainous island had initially been put to the Count, his response was that there were no roads. Undeterred by this minor obstacle, the organisers found a tortuous 90 mile (145km) loop which proved more than a match for man and machine. Following a 12-year absence, the race was revived in 1919 over the 67 mile (108km) Madonie circuit. This may have been of a lesser distance than the original but the mountain twists ensured that there was no shortage of hazards. Among the 25 starters were a number of interesting names. Enzo Ferrari was making his racing debut at the wheel of a CMN; graduating from hill climbs, Antonio Ascari, the new hope of Italy, was driving a Fiat; André Boillot, younger brother of Georges who had been killed in the First World War, was in a 2.5-litre Peugeot; and René Thomas was driving an Indianapolis Ballot car which had been entered so late that Thomas had been obliged to drive it all the way from Paris to Naples. At one point on the journey through Italy Thomas had to wait while scaffolding was erected to replace a stretch of road that had been washed away by torrential rain. Most of the starters were Italian, including the Alfa Romeos of Giuseppe Campari and Nino Franchini and the pair of 1914 Grand Prix Fiats driven by Ascari and Count Giulio Masetti.

Thomas may have been forgiven for thinking that he had seen off the worst of the weather in Italy but on the eve of the race a raging storm deposited a 2in (5.1cm) covering of snow on the mountain section. The following morning at 7a.m. Enzo Ferrari was first away, followed by Ascari, in a devilish combination of snow and high winds, swiftly followed by rain, hail, sleet and sun, although not always in that order. To cope with the conditions, the drivers wore gauze masks but discarded their goggles because of the snow. The principal casualty on the first lap was Ascari, whose Fiat skidded on the treacherous road, plunged down a 30-foot ravine and was not found until halfway through the race! André Boillot was proving a worthy successor to his illustrious brother and an opening lap of 1hr 54min 36sec gave him a lead of nearly four minutes over Thomas, with Domenico Gambino third in a Diatto and Count Masetti's Fiat in fourth. But starting the second lap Boillot's Peugeot skidded, struck a bank, leapt 3ft (0.9m) in the air, dropped on two wheels and was only prevented from plunging 200ft (61m) over a precipice by a handily placed pile of stones. A lesser driver might have been unnerved by this experience but Boillot pushed on regardless, maintaining a healthy lead over Thomas despite having a car which boasted just half of his rival's cubic capacity.

When Thomas came in for fuel at the start of the final lap, having driven flat out, he discovered to his horror that he was still seven minutes behind. Boillot's carefree approach to this treacherous circuit had seen him leave the road on no fewer than six occasions but between accidents he was by far the quickest driver in the race. He didn't even bother to stop for fuel when beginning the last lap. Instead his equally manic mechanic grabbed a can from the pits and refuelled on the move. Thomas pressed on boldly but couldn't hope to compete with such daredevil tactics and in the end he pushed too hard and crashed, leaving Boillot with a lead of around half an hour.

Others might have been content to coast home but the Frenchman continued to drive like a madman right to the finish. It very nearly proved his undoing. For as news reached the crowd in the stands of Boillot's impending arrival, knots of spectators began to trickle excitedly on to the circuit. Boillot came roaring round the final corner and suddenly saw hordes of people in front of him. He jammed on the brakes and swerved to avoid the clusters of well-wishers but merely succeeded in spinning into the grandstand ... just 10 yards (9.1m) from the finish. Perhaps feeling guilty at their part in the proceedings (although three of their number were injured in the collision), the spectators started to push Boillot's car back on to the track until a journalist helpfully pointed out that Boillot would be disqualified unless he and his mechanic did the pushing. Although in the latter stages of exhaustion, the pair succeeded in dragging the battered Peugeot back on to the road, from where Boillot rolled across the finish line backwards. But that wasn't the end of it. Ernest Ballot reminded them that reversing over the finish line was also illegal so they were lifted back into the car, drove down the road, turned round and this time crossed the line facing the right way. A yard or so over the line, Boillot collapsed over the wheel, muttering gloriously, *'C'est pour la France!'*

His average speed of 34⅕mph (55km/h) had spread-eagled the field. Antonio Moriondo's Itala finished second, half an hour adrift, and Gamboni was a further 12 minutes back in third. Enzo Ferrari completed the race (no mean achievement in itself) but was well down the field. On the day nobody could cope with the new Boillot.

A PIT STOP FOR LUNCH
EUROPEAN GRAND PRIX, 29 JUNE 1925

The first Grand Prix to be staged in Belgium was held at the 8¾ mile (14km) Spa circuit in 1925. A race had been scheduled for 1914 but by then a different sort of battle was being fought on Belgian soil. The 1925 event was run under the title of the European Grand Prix but a low turnout and a monotonous race was scarcely the best advert for European motor racing. In fact the day was memorable for just one reason – the most amazing display of arrogance by the Alfa Romeo team. If you can imagine Michael Schumacher prolonging a pit stop to tuck into a picnic, you'll get the picture.

Twelve cars were supposed to take part but when the Sunbeams and Guyots scratched, that left four Delages against three Alfas. The Delage drivers were René Thomas, Robert Benoist, Albert Divo and Paul Torchy, while the Alfa team comprised Antonio Ascari, Giuseppe Campari and Count Gastone Brilli-Peri. There should have been everything to play for since, although the World Championship did not begin in earnest until 1950, a short-lived experiment did take place for manufacturers from 1925, and this was one of the races which counted, in company with the Indianapolis 500 and the French and Italian Grands Prix. The other innovation for the year was the abolition of riding mechanics in Grand Prix events. Most racing cars now became single-seaters.

Ascari led the way round the first lap from Campari, Benoist, Brilli-Peri, Divo, Torchy and Thomas but on the next Benoist dropped out with a split fuel tank. On lap four Torchy stopped for new plugs and retired soon after. The Delage misery deepened three laps later when Thomas's car caught fire. He burnt his left hand trying to beat out the flames and retired. So after little more than 50 (80.5) of the 500 miles (805km), there were only four cars left running.

At half-distance Ascari was still showing the way to Campari, Divo and Brilli-Peri. It was hardly riveting entertainment for the Belgian crowd but it was to get much, much worse. For soon Brilli-Peri retired with a broken spring and Divo exited the race after making two long stops – one for tyres, the other for plugs. Now it was just the two Alfas. Round and round they went, separated by over a quarter of an hour. The crowd, partly disappointed at the lack of French involvement but even more disgruntled by the tedious procession, began to jeer and boo the Alfa drivers. Irked by this show of disapproval, Alfa team manager Vittorio Jano decided to rub in the Italian superiority by arranging for a sumptuous lunch to be laid out in the pits. Then, to a crescendo of boos and hisses, he called in his two drivers and they sat down to a leisurely meal while the mechanics polished the cars. The spectators could hardly believe their eyes.

Their stomachs satisfied, Ascari and Campari resumed the 'race', remaining in that order to the finish at which point Ascari was 22 minutes ahead of his team-mate. He had led from start to finish at an average speed of 74½mph (119.9km/h).

The joy of Ascari and Alfa was to be short-lived. He was killed in his next major event, the French Grand Prix, following which the Alfa cars withdrew from the race as a mark of respect. Alfa still won that inaugural World Constructors' Championship (beating Duesenberg and Bugatti), but the season had been tarnished by the death of their star driver. It was all a far cry from that picnic in the pits at Spa.

A CLASH OF THE GIANTS
BROOKLANDS MATCH,
11 JULY 1925

Parry Thomas knew every inch of Brooklands and particularly its famous banking. A wheel mark made by him in 1925 was just 2in (5.1cm) from the top of the banking, while on another occasion he got so close to the edge that his car removed a shrub growing on the other side. His formidable Leyland-Thomas machine was a match for any vehicle over a short distance of the Surrey circuit and held the lap record at more than 120mph (193km/h). In 1923 he issued a challenge to any driver for a race over three or four laps, but there were no takers. However a handicapped standing-lap contest was run one moonlit Thursday evening between Thomas, George Duller's Bugatti and Ernest Eldridge's mighty 21.7-litre Fiat 'Mephistopheles', which was fitted with an airship engine and had frightening speed and power in short bursts. With only the exhaust flames of the cars visible to spectators, the Leyland gave a five-second start to the Fiat and 30 seconds to the Bugatti but crossed the line 30 yards (27.4m) ahead of Duller with Eldridge just behind in third. Thomas reissued the challenge in 1924 and Eldridge was all set to race him at that year's autumn meeting until the Fiat broke an oil pump in practice.

The match was rescheduled for the West Kent Motor Club meeting in the summer of 1925 over three laps, for stakes of £500. Since it was just a small club meeting, fewer than 2,000 people turned up to watch one of Brooklands' greatest duels. Eldridge drove without helmet or goggles but did take the precaution of carrying a passenger to warn him when Thomas was trying to overtake. Thomas wore his customary Fair Isle jersey, helmet and goggles. The two huge machines started together from the 1 mile (1.6km) box on the railway straight with Thomas on the inside. *The Autocar* recounted the contest in less than glowing terms. 'A more horrid spectacle to sit and watch has probably never been seen in motor racing. Several well-known drivers hurried to the bar, at which they remained out of sight, full of apprehension, until the race was over.'

As the flag fell, the Leyland took a lead of a length, to the astonishment of most onlookers, but before the half mile (0.8km) the chain-driven Fiat accelerated and had surged into a lead of 200 yards (183m) by the Byfleet banking, which it took in a typically flamboyant skid. When the Fiat again swerved near the Fork, trackside spectators fled for cover. Thomas closed a little but an attempt at passing was thwarted when the Leyland slid down the banking. Eldridge adopted the tactic of keeping the Fiat low on the banking sections and, despite a succession of hair-raising skids, was able to maintain his slender advantage starting the third and final lap. The Fiat still looked the likely winner but as it slewed across the Fork for the final time, the engine cut out, allowing the Leyland to thunder past. Any doubt regarding the outcome was settled on the Members' banking when the Fiat's off-side rear tyre blew, sending chunks of rubber flying over the tree tops. Eldridge pressed on but Thomas claimed the spoils at an average of 123¼mph (198.3km/h) as opposed to the Fiat's 121⅕mph (195km/h). Thomas also set a new lap record of 129⁷⁄₁₀mph (208.7km/h). Brooklands had never seen anything quite like it.

THREE CAR TRICK

LE MANS 24-HOUR RACE,
18 JUNE 1927

The cathedral city of Le Mans in north-west France had been to the forefront of European motor racing since staging the inaugural French Grand Prix in 1906, on a circuit to the east of the city. Between 1911 and 1913 the Grand Prix de France (an event not to be confused with the French Grand Prix) was held on a long, triangular circuit to the south of Le Mans and after the war sections of this route were incorporated in a new 10¾ mile (17.3km) layout. This track, which consisted of public roads including part of Route Nationale 158 (the main Le Mans-Tours highway), provided a splendid setting for the 1921 French Grand Prix and encouraged thoughts of a long-distance race to demonstrate the reliability of touring cars. The Bol d'Or 24-hour race for light cars had been held at St Germain, near Paris, in 1922, proving that it was possible to stage night races other than in floodlit stadiums. And so in 1923 the Le Mans 24-Hour Race was born.

For the 1927 event, the British challenge was spearheaded by three big green Bentleys whose noisy exhausts shook the surrounding French countryside. Bentley had won in 1924 and had come so close two years later, only for S.C.H. (Sammy) Davis to drive the car into a sandbank when trying to regain second spot with just half an hour remaining. Given a lift back to the pits, he was faced with the unwelcome task of reporting the mishap to W.O. Bentley. Davis later

wrote: 'I went for a long walk alone, and wished I was dead.'
But Davis was back in the same 3-litre car – the famous 'Old
No. 7' – and was joined in the team by Leslie Callingham (in
a powerful 4.5-litre model) and George Duller. Only 22 cars
lined up for the start, partly because tougher regulations
regarding refuelling had deterred the leading French teams
of La Lorraine and Chenard-Walcker from taking part, and
also because the entire Tracta team had gone joy-riding the
night before, resulting in a crash which put most of them in
hospital. One of the team who was passed fit, Grégoire, was
conspicuous for two reasons: his Tracta was the first front-
drive car ever to appear in a competition, and he drove with
a huge bandage around his head, a legacy of the inadvisable
night out.

Four o'clock sharp saw the traditional Le Mans start
(introduced in 1925) whereby the drivers ran across
the track to their cars. Those whose vehicles possessed
convertible tops had the added chore of having to raise the
hood before driving off. As expected, Callingham's monster
Bentley set the pace and was comfortably ahead of his two
team-mates when, an hour after dusk, a single crash at
White House took out the entire Bentley team.

Callingham came roaring into the corner at over 70mph
(112.6km/h) to find a Schneider broadside across the track.
Unable to avoid it, he crashed into it, spun and rolled across
the road into a ditch on the far side. Seconds later, Duller,
who was two laps behind, appeared on the scene. A noted
amateur steeplechase jockey, he chose to jump for his
life when he saw what was about to happen. He managed
to avoid the Schneider but smashed into Callingham's
car. Davis, in the third Bentley, had deliberately dropped
back a little as darkness fell to avoid dazzling Duller with
his headlights. He saw Duller's car ahead rush down the
hill, jump the bridge and disappear round the bend. Davis
wrote: 'As I swung around that right hand turn, on the road
was a scatter of earth, a piece or two of splintered wood.

The thing flashed an immediate warning ... but even then it did not occur to me to do more than slow down a little and be ready. The car swung round White House Corner almost at full speed. I jammed down the brake pedal, tried to spin the wheel and skidded broadside on, for, white and horrible in the headlights' beam, an appalling tangle of smashed cars appeared right across the road in front! With the rending crash of riven metal, we slid right into the mess, with a shock that threw me hard against the wheel. All the lights went out.' As Davis clambered out, he saw that the 'mess' was one Bentley on its side with the other on top of it. The three Bentley drivers, dazed but otherwise unhurt, stood there momentarily in the finest British stiff upper-lip tradition discussing the best course of action. The cars of Callingham and Duller were beyond redemption but Davis managed to extricate his machine from the tangled heap of metal and limp back to the pits. Moments after he had left White House, another car ploughed into the wreckage.

The damage to Davis's car included a bent front axle and frame, a smashed mudguard and running board, and a broken headlight. By the time a wheel had been replaced, a new headlamp had been fitted, the battery box had been secured firmly and the running board had been strapped up, half an hour had elapsed. With co-driver Dr Dudley Benjafield at the wheel, the patched-up Bentley set off in pursuit of the new leading car, the 3-litre Aries of Jean Chassagne and Laly. In pouring rain, Benjafield made considerable inroads, gaining a whole lap. But at 2.30 on the Sunday afternoon – with just 90 minutes to go – the Bentley was still a lap behind when 'Doc' Benjafield spotted the Aries stopped at the side of the road near Mulsanne. The following lap it was still there. The Aries was out of the race with fuel pump failure. Incredibly, magically, the battered Bentley was in the lead. And there it stayed, Davis bringing it home – mudguards flapping in the wind – to a memorable triumph by 217 miles (349.2km). Only seven cars finished. After the winners had been deluged with flowers and soaked in champagne, Davis discovered that the link arm to the steering had all but sheared through and that a mere ¼in (0.6cm) of damaged metal had stood between victory and tragedy. For had the link arm parted at 90mph (144.8km/h), the driver would almost certainly have been killed.

The Bentley legend was confirmed at the celebration dinner at London's Savoy Hotel. With a straight face, chairman Sir Edward Iliffe rose to announce that a lady who was entitled to be at the dinner was waiting outside, and invited her to enter. The folding doors were swung back and, with her one headlamp blazing, No. 7 roared into the room for the grandest of entrances. The only people not amused were the Savoy management who had reacted in horror to the sight of the famous Bentley Boys manhandling the old lady up the hotel stairs!

THE ACTRESS AND THE OPERA SINGER

MILLE MIGLIA, 13 APRIL 1929

Count Aymo Maggi had dreamed of making his home town of Brescia the focus of the world's greatest motor race. Together with fellow Brescia residents, Count Franco Mazzotti, Renzo Castegneto and Giovanni Canestrini, Maggi conceived the idea of a 1,000 mile (1,609km) race through Italy, starting and finishing in Brescia, and taking place on public roads which would not officially be closed for the duration. The ambitious proposal appealed to Italian leader Benito Mussolini, who saw motor racing as the way forward, and in 1927 the first Mille Miglia was held. It quickly lived up to its billing as the finest road race in the world.

The first two Mille Miglias had been a resounding success, happily free from the accidents which had plagued the inter-city races at the turn of the century and which some had predicted would blight this charge through the towns and villages of northern and central Italy. Not only did the races attract sizeable entries but they made the sport accessible to the Italian people, who turned up in their thousands along the route to cheer on their favourites. The 1929 race attracted a more modest 72 entries, mainly because it clashed with the Monaco Grand Prix, which was considered the major event by the motoring world. With eight Bugattis at Monte Carlo, there were none left for the Mille Miglia. Indeed there were no foreign works entries, making the strong Alfa Romeo team hot favourites, their challenge spearheaded by the victorious 1928 pairing of Giuseppe Campari and Giulio Ramponi. Campari was a larger than life character. A frustrated opera singer, he loved to sing at the top of his voice while roaring along the road. Alfa's chief rivals were the Brescia-based OM team, whose drivers included Antonio Brivio and the up-and-coming Tazio Nuvolari. The smaller classes were expected to be dominated by the Fiat 509s who made up more than a quarter of the total entry. The most colourful competitor was actress Mimi Aylmer, who arrived at the start wearing a smart red dress and fur jacket, with her chauffeur at the wheel of a Lancia Lamba. Everyone assumed that the chauffeur would do the driving but at the last minute she took the wheel, relegating him to the passenger seat where he was to stay for the entire race. Ahead of them all lay 1,018 miles (1,638km) spread over two days, the route descending as far south as Rome. At least one third of the race would be run on dirt roads, additional hazards including 67 level crossings, many of which were unmanned.

Surprisingly it was the lone Maserati of 'Baconin' Borzacchini and Ernesto Maserati which led to Bologna, by which time the OM driven by two of the race founders, Maggi and Mazzotti, had been forced to retire with transmission trouble. Another early casualty was Nuvolari, who crashed out in what would subsequently prove to be typically spectacular style. Four minutes behind the Maserati was Campari, pursued by Achille Varzi, Count Brilli-Peri and Carlo Pintacuda, all in Alfas. On the run down to Rome Varzi was delayed for half an hour by having to stop and put out a fire, and Brilli-Peri dropped out with engine trouble. Borzacchini and Maserati were still ahead at Rome but on the notoriously tricky drive up to the Adriatic, they dropped out with transmission trouble. This seemed to leave the way clear for Alfa and by the time they reached the Adriatic coast Campari and Ramponi held a lead of over

20 minutes. Back at Bologna, with just a fifth of the race to go, Campari still had a commanding advantage over the OM of Giuseppe Morandi and Archimede Rosa, which had moved up into second ahead of Varzi. Although Campari's car suffered two punctures on the final section, he reached Brescia to win by ten minutes from Morandi and Rosa with Varzi and Colombo two minutes behind in third. The Alfa's winning time was 18hr 4min 25sec, an average speed of 56 $\frac{1}{20}$mph (90.2km/h). Forty-two of the 72 starters were still going at the finish.

Among them was Mimi Aylmer, but not until she had made one last gesture to her adoring fans. Way down the field in twenty-ninth place and some seven hours behind the winner, she pulled over on the outskirts of Brescia and stopped for five minutes to attend to her hair and make-up. After putting on fresh lipstick, she felt able to face her public once more and drove on to the finish where she received a rapturous welcome. She then stepped out of the car with a radiant smile, immaculately groomed, and showing no sign whatsoever of fatigue. The expression on her chauffeur's face told a different story. Looking a nervous wreck, the poor man was later given a special award at the prize-giving for being the most courageous man of the race. Without doubt he had earned it.

THE ICE-MAN MELTETH

TARGA FLORIO, 4 MAY 1930

Achille Varzi was known as the ice-man of Italian motor racing. Whereas fellow countryman and fierce rival, Tazio Nuvolari, typified the explosive Latin temperament, Varzi remained cool and calculating. This approach had brought Varzi a number of victories in minor races but he had yet to establish himself in the very top flight of world drivers. At the 1930 Mille Miglia the flamboyant Nuvolari had revelled in emphasising his superiority. Well ahead on time as dawn was about to break on the second day, he spotted Varzi ahead of him on the road. Switching off his lights, he crept up on Varzi unawares, then flashed them on again as he swept past on his way to victory. For Varzi it had been a humiliating experience. Nuvolari was the top dog ... and both men knew it.

Three weeks later the pair met again in the Targa Florio, run over five laps of the intimidating Madonie circuit. The Alfa Romeo team was managed by Enzo Ferrari, who had cars for Nuvolari, Giuseppe Campari and Varzi. The last-named had driven a modified Alfa P2 to victory in the Bordino Prize at Alessandria but, with a top speed of 140mph (225.3km/h), it was considered unsuited to the twisting Madonie course. Ferrari certainly thought so and warned Varzi that the car was too dangerous for the Targa Florio, but Varzi put his foot down. Campari and Nuvolari were not exactly renowned for erring on the side of caution but even they steered clear of the P2 for this race, preferring instead to drive two of the new 1,750cc sports cars. Bugatti sent a strong four-man team, led by Louis Chiron and Albert Divo, and there was also stiff opposition from the Maseratis of Luigi Arcangeli, Baconin Borzacchini and Ernesto Maserati, but this was to be the day that Achille Varzi came of age.

He announced his intentions from the off, putting in a blistering opening lap to break the track record and lead the way from Nuvolari and Campari in the other Alfas and the Bugatti trio of Chiron, Divo and Count Carlo Alberto Conelli. Chiron upped the tempo to overtake Nuvolari and Campari on elapsed time but, at the end of the second lap, was still losing ground to the seemingly unstoppable Varzi. On the third lap, however, Varzi suffered a fuel leak which allowed Chiron to close the gap to less than two minutes, and when the Italian came into the pits for a wheel change at the end of lap four, he was actually half a minute behind. Having started 12 minutes behind Chiron, he was unaware of the problems that the Monegasque driver was encountering out on the circuit, for Chiron had skidded on some loose stones on a downhill section and had been forced to change two wheels. But for Varzi back in the pits every second counted. There was no time for a longer stop to take on fuel so his riding mechanic snatched the can and proceeded to pour the fuel into the tank as the car sped off along the road. In doing so, he spilt some on to the exhaust. Within an instant, flames were licking around Varzi's neck but he had come too close to victory to be denied now and, keeping his legendary cool, he drove on defiantly while the mechanic valiantly tried to beat down the flames with a seat cushion. Somehow they negotiated that final lap safely and speedily, and took the chequered flag to wild cheers from the patriotic Sicilian crowd. Chiron was nearly two minutes back in second with Conelli third, Campari fourth and Nuvolari only fifth. Varzi had well and truly proved his point. Both he and the car had been up to the task. He was now able to join the world's racing élite.

FAGIOLI BRINGS THE BRIDGE DOWN

CZECHOSLOVAKIAN GRAND PRIX, 27 SEPTEMBER 1931

The 18⅕ mile (29.3km) Masaryk circuit at Brno in Czechoslovakia was used occasionally during the 1930s and was the setting for a remarkable national event in 1931 which featured just about the most unusual accident in Grand Prix history.

A sizeable crowd turned up to watch the 308 mile (496km) race, among them Czech driver Elisabeth Junek, whose participation in the 1928 Targa Florio had created a sensation when it became known that the race leader for a short while was a woman. She also raced in that year's German Grand Prix, sharing the driving with husband Vincenz (the owner of one of Prague's premier banking houses), but he suffered a fatal accident in the race, after which his wife retired from competitive driving.

Luigi Fagioli was first away at Brno in a Maserati, pulling out a useful lead on the opening lap from Baconin Borzacchini, Achille Varzi, Rudolf Caracciola, Louis Chiron and Tazio Nuvolari. Fagioli was still in the lead on lap two when the rear hub cap of his car struck one of the pillars of a temporary wooden bridge which had been erected across the circuit and brought the entire bridge crashing down on to the track in front of his pursuers. Varzi, who had moved up to second, took the main brunt but managed to bulldoze his way miraculously through the fallen timber. However, his efforts proved in vain, having caused so much damage to the front axle of his Bugatti that he had to retire. Nuvolari collided with the timbers a few seconds later and broke the rear axle of his Alfa. While Varzi drove Nuvolari back to the pits, Fagioli also had to drop out on the next lap as a result of the curious collision, which mercifully did not result in any injuries to drivers or spectators.

Shortly afterwards Marcel Lehoux hit a boundary stone and broke a wheel rim. Changing the wheel, he set off again to such good effect that he broke the lap record, only to retire immediately afterwards with a bent differential shaft. Next to suffer was Caracciola, whose big Mercedes hit a marker post and wrecked the near-side wheel. This chapter of accidents left Louis Chiron's Bugatti with an unassailable advantage and, although Fagioli switched to a second Maserati and Nuvolari replaced Borzacchini, neither could catch the leaders. Chiron eventually won by nearly a lap from Hans Stuck's Mercedes, with German driver Heinrich-Joachim von Morgen third in a Bugatti. Chiron's third win of the season had certainly been his most eventful.

VICTORY AT 1½MPH
MONTE CARLO RALLY, JANUARY 1932

After travelling the length or breadth of Europe through snow and ice as quickly as was humanly and mechanically possible, competitors in the 1932 Monte Carlo Rally found that the entire event would be decided by a crazy final test in which they had to drive as *slowly* as they could over a distance of 100 yards (91.4m). The rules stipulated that during the test the wheels had to be moving at all times. Although nobody else liked the innovation, it seemed to suit M. Vasselle, whose 3.5-litre Hotchkiss saloon covered the 100 yards in 2min 35.51sec at a speed of 1½mph (2.4km/h) to win the most coveted prize in rallying. No wonder the next day's headlines were along the lines of: 'FARCICAL TEST RUINS MONTE CARLO RALLY'.

The Monte had first been run in 1911 and each winter saw cars converging on Monaco from all over Europe. For 1932 there was a new starting point, Umea in northern Sweden, 2,231 miles (3,950km) from Monte Carlo. Since the object of the exercise was for competitors to cover the greatest distance possible within the time limits, Umea became a popular choice, with over half of the 116 entrants opting to start from there. In the end, the top 18 all started from Umea. Among them were Vasselle and the 1931 winner, Donald Healey, who was driving an Invicta. By contrast, only eight crews decided to set off from Athens even though it was actually 21 miles (33.8km) further from Monaco. But no driver had yet managed to battle his way through the snows of Yugoslavia in January. Other starting points that year included Frankfurt, Gibraltar, John O'Groats, Lisbon, Stavanger, Jassy, Palermo and Glasgow. The most unusual starter from Glasgow was Rootes PR man Dudley Noble in a Hillman Wizard 75 ... towing a caravan.

Although the Umea starters had to cope with black ice and three ferry crossings, 28 made it to Monte. Even Vasselle's car, which had a top speed of just 50mph (80.5km/h), went off the road at one point. The conditions in the Balkans were no better than usual, yet five cars from Athens managed to force their way through. Indeed the starters who fared worst were those who had set off from John O'Groats. They were severely hampered by widespread flooding.

Of course reaching Monaco was one thing. Now they had to face the deciding test. The previous year's braking and acceleration test had been scrapped and replaced by this new curious examination of driving skills. Cars had to be driven as slowly as possible, in top gear, for 100 yards, then as fast as possible (still in top gear) over the next 100 yards, at the end of which they had to be stopped within 40 yards (36.6m). Many competitors prepared for the test by calling in at local garages for wheels or axle ratios to be changed. This apparently took the rally organisers by surprise. Healey had small spare wheels fitted to his Invicta immediately before the test so that the rear of the car almost scraped along the ground. It had the desired effect, enabling Healey to record a slow time of 1min 54.91sec – good enough for second place overall. However, he was too quick for Vasselle who thus became the first – and only – man to win the Monte by driving slowly. For the following year the ill-conceived go-slow test was unceremoniously dumped.

CAMPARI'S HAMMER BLOW

MILLE MIGLIA, 9 APRIL 1932

Giuseppe Campari was the undisputed king of the Mille Miglia. The winner in 1928 and 1929, third in 1930 and second in 1931, he was expected to make another bold show in the 1932 race, particularly since he was at the wheel of one of the all-conquering Alfa Romeos. In recent years the event had virtually turned into an Alfa benefit and in 1932 the company provided almost half of the entire 88-car entry. There were works cars for Campari, Rudolf Caracciola, Baconin Borzacchini and Tazio Nuvolari, supplemented by several Scuderia Ferrari Alfas entered by Enzo Ferrari and driven by the likes of Pietro and Mario Ghersi, Giulio Ramponi, Carlo Trossi, Antonio Brivio and Piero Taruffi. One man sadly missing from the Alfa line-up was Luigi Arcangeli who had been killed at Monza while practising for the previous year's Italian Grand Prix. The serious opposition to Alfa was pretty much confined to Achille Varzi in a Bugatti and the Lancia Lambda of Strazza and Gismondi, although there were interesting entries from a couple of English aristocrats – Lord de Clifford in a 750cc MG Midget and the Hon. Brian Lewis (later Lord Essendon) at the wheel of a Talbot 105.

On the first section to Bologna, Nuvolari led from Varzi and Caracciola, with just five seconds covering them, and all three averaging over 100mph (160.9km/h) for the stage, but as the cars took to the mountains Varzi sustained a hole in his petrol tank and retired. Approaching Florence, Pietro Ghersi tried to take a sharp bend too fast and skidded into a lamp-post, wrecking the car. A few minutes later the cheering crowd welcomed the 1930 winner Nuvolari but, spotting the bent Alfa, his attention wandered for a split second, which was long enough for him to crash into a tree, his car coming to rest a matter of yards from Ghersi's. The impact of the accident was so severe that Nuvolari's co-driver, Gianbattista Guidotti, was thrown from the car and knocked unconscious. When Guidotti eventually came round, there was no sign of Nuvolari, but he was vaguely aware of being carried on a stretcher by four sinister-looking figures wearing long, flowing cloaks with hoods over their heads. Dazed and confused, Guidotti feared he was being abducted by the Ku Klux Klan, so he closed his eyes and pretended to be dead. Only later did he discover that his 'abductors' were dedicated Florentine monks who were taking him to the monastery hospital for treatment. Another early casualty was Giacomo Ragnoli, who was making his race debut in a Fiat. Heading south from Bologna on the road to Florence, his car veered off the road on a bend. Ragnoli was unharmed and walked into an inn, conveniently located on the offending corner, and downed several brandies. In the following year's race he went off at the same corner ...

At Florence it was Caracciola who led from Campari and Taruffi, and the positions remained unaltered down to Rome except that Campari and Taruffi swapped places. Crossing the Apennines, Caracciola lost valuable time when he was forced to stop to adjust his brakes and by the time he reached Terni, the German's lead over Taruffi had been cut to a minute with Campari a further minute adrift in third. Campari began to scent another famous victory and overhauled Taruffi, so that by Perugia he was just 35 seconds behind Caracciola with Borzacchini moving up to third. Building up a veritable head of steam, the burly

Campari powered on and had surged into the lead as he approached the Adriatic coast. However, such flat-out driving over winding roads had taken its toll and Campari decided to let his mechanic, Sozzi, have a turn at the wheel so that the great man could take a breather in preparation for the final assault. No sooner had Sozzi taken over than he crashed the Alfa into a wall near Ancona and put himself and Campari out of the race. Perhaps understandably, Campari was not best pleased and chased the tearful Sozzi down the road brandishing a hammer from the tool kit. Fortunately for Sozzi, while he may not have been the faster driver, he was the faster runner.

Campari's mishap left Borzacchini in the lead and he pulled out a ten-minute advantage over the ailing Caracciola, who was soon to retire with a cracked chassis. The Alfa of Taruffi and Eugenio Siena gave chase before falling victim to a broken piston near Bologna. This allowed Trossi and Brivio to claim second place, eventually finishing 15 minutes behind the winning car of Borzacchini and Bignami. A total of 42 cars made it back to Brescia with Alfa filling nine of the first ten places, only being denied a clean sweep by the Strazza/ Gismondi Lancia which came seventh. Down in twenty-fifth was the Hon. Brian Lewis who, after already losing time by taking a wrong turning, had to resort to patching up a holed fuel tank with a piece of chewing gum.

So Borzacchini was the toast of Brescia that night ... but Campari maintained with some justification that victory should have been his.

A FIERY FINISH
MONACO GRAND PRIX, 23 APRIL 1933

The first Monaco Grand Prix in 1929 had been hailed by bewildered observers as 'the nearest approach to a Roman chariot race that has been seen of recent years'. With its glamorous Riviera backdrop and spectators afforded unrivalled, close-up views of the action, it quickly became an immensely popular addition to the racing year, and in 1933 broke new ground by being the first Grand Prix at which grid positions were decided on practice times rather than by ballot. The race itself would go down in history as the scene of one of the greatest duels of all time, between those old foes Achille Varzi and Tazio Nuvolari, and one which, even after 99 laps of non-stop cut and thrust, still managed to provide a sensational sting in the tail.

The practice sessions were dramatic enough. Rudolf Caracciola ploughed into a wall, badly injuring his right leg – an accident which kept him out of racing for over a year and left him with a permanent limp. And Nuvolari completed only 11 practice laps before bending his car so badly at Sainte Devote that it was not repaired until race day. The all-important times produced a front row of Varzi (Bugatti), Louis Chiron (Alfa Romeo) and Baconin Borzacchini (Alfa Romeo). Nuvolari's Alfa was on the second row. The Alfa was faster than the Bugatti in a straight line but there aren't too many of those at Monaco, where the Bugatti's superior cornering was expected to come into its own.

From the inside berth, Varzi shot into the lead on the first of the 100 laps, ahead of Borzacchini, Marcel Lehoux and Nuvolari. On lap two Nuvolari moved up into second and next time round he edged into the lead. For the next 50 laps the pair exchanged leadership of the race with bewildering regularity, there rarely being more than a second between the two cars. The pace they set was so furious that the first of the back-markers was lapped after just seven circuits. Behind the two leaders was an equally ferocious scrap for third spot between the Alfas of Borzacchini and Philippe Etancelin, but then the flamboyant Frenchman skidded at the chicane, allowing Borzacchini to pull clear. Etancelin pressed on and broke Varzi's lap record on lap 51, eventually catching Borzacchini seven laps later. But then on lap 65 Etancelin's axle shaft broke, putting him out of the race.

This battle, however, paled into insignificance alongside the one which continued unabated for the lead. Nuvolari was driving in typically demonic fashion, taking corners with just one hand on the wheel because the other was almost constantly occupied with the gear lever. Although he had managed to maintain his narrow advantage for much of the race, the lead continued to change hands frequently and on lap 80 Varzi got past once more. On lap 83, Nuvolari led; by lap 93, it was Varzi; on lap 98 – with just two remaining – it was Nuvolari. With no more than a car's length separating them, they sped around the world's tightest and trickiest circuit as if joined by an invisible piece of string. Before the end of lap 99, Varzi had seized the initiative (setting a new lap record in the process), only to be re-passed at the beginning of the final lap. Surely now Nuvolari would hold on, but as the pair went up the hill to the Casino for the last time, smoke was seen pouring from the Alfa's bonnet. An oil pipe had burst as a result of Nuvolari over-revving on the hill. Varzi gratefully accepted the invitation and shot by to record a memorable victory.

Meanwhile Nuvolari coasted grimly on towards the finish

until the hot oil caused a fire. As flames shot out from beneath the Alfa's bonnet, he jumped from the burning car and pushed it across the finish line, hotly pursued by irate officials waving fire extinguishers. Unfortunately one of the Alfa crew also lent a hand, which resulted in Nuvolari being disqualified, second place going to Borzacchini and third to René Dreyfus in a Bugatti. So the little man had nothing to show for what was, even by his standards, an inspired drive. Of the 100 laps, he had led for 64 and Varzi for only 36, but on the vital last lap Lady Luck had chosen to side with Varzi.

ON THE BEACH

SOUTHPORT SANDS 50-MILE RACE, 29 APRIL 1933

Throughout the 1920s and 1930s race meetings and record attempts were popular fixtures on spacious beaches all over Britain – notably at places such as Pendine, Porthcawl, Saltburn, Weston-super-Mare, Skegness and Southport where the tide being out guaranteed miles of sand on which to lay out a course or attain extraordinarily high speeds. That is not to say that beach racing was all plain sailing. The tide came in so fast at a Skegness meeting in 1924 that the last race of the afternoon was reported as being run with the course awash. Another hazard was that in races of several laps the sandy corners would become badly churned up by successive cars, making it difficult for drivers to pick a smooth path or maintain control of their machines. At Southport one year May Cunliffe became 'tramlined' in such ruts in her super charged Sunbeam, as a result of which the car rolled over and over, killing her father who was acting as riding mechanic.

Southport Motor Club called itself the World's Premier Beach Racing Club and regularly attracted crowds in excess of 15,000, all kept under control by mounted police. Among its finest coups was attracting a visit from speed king Sir Henry O'Neal de Hane Segrave for a meeting in September 1925. Segrave, winner of the 1923 French Grand Prix, drove a 2-litre red Sunbeam and proved just as unbeatable on Birkdale Sands as he had at Tours. At the end of the day he had won 11 races and four cups, including the prestigious 10 mile (16.1km) event. And in one of the speed trials for which he would later become famous, he thrilled the spectators by reaching a speed of over 100mph (160.9km/h). He did, however, lose out in a match with C.M. Needham's Brough Superior motorcycle, run over 1 mile (1.6km) from a standing start. Needham won by inches after Segrave had hit a soft patch of sand while trying to accelerate away from the start. Such were the vagaries of beach racing.

In April 1933 Birkdale Sands staged a 50 mile (80.5km) race over 100 laps of a short circuit divided down the middle by a row of flags so that the cars had to negotiate a hairpin bend at either end. With some 3,000 cars parked on the beach to watch, the race developed into a battle between the Bugattis and the smaller, more manoeuvrable, supercharged Austin Sevens which, on account of their lesser engine capacities, were given four credit laps. This proved decisive as W.L. Thompson's Austin Seven held on gamely to win from the early leader, Jack Field's Bugatti. As the mighty Bugatti crossed the finish line, the exertion of so much tight cornering took its toll and the piston collapsed, sending clouds of smoke into the air. Marshals ran amok with fire extinguishers and Field emerged unharmed, none the worse for his day on the beach.

THE FIXED RACE
TRIPOLI GRAND PRIX, 7 MAY 1933

The 1933 Tripoli Grand Prix should be remembered for a gallant – and ultimately tragic – final drive by that dashing Englishman Sir Henry 'Tim' Birkin. Instead it is better known as being the subject of the great Grand Prix fixing scandal, the result of the race allegedly rigged by the leading Italian drivers so that they could profit from the State Lottery.

The newly opened Melaha circuit at Tripoli was 8½ miles (13.7km) long and the fastest in the world. Speeds of up to 140mph (225.3km/h) were commonplace. With Libya then an Italian colony, that great motor racing fan, Mussolini, wanted maximum publicity for the circuit and the race. To this end, Marshal Balbo, the new governor of Libya, organised a national lottery in conjunction with the Grand Prix. Tickets went on sale in Italy months before the race. For the layout of no more than a few lire, there was the prospect of winning seven and a half million lire, the equivalent of around £80,000. This was serious money. Three days before the race, 30 lucky tickets were drawn – one for each of the starters.

On the eve of the race a stout, bald-headed gentleman called at Achille Varzi's hotel room. He introduced himself as Enrico Rivio, a timber merchant from Pisa, and explained that he had drawn the lottery ticket bearing the number of Varzi's car. He asked Varzi to win the race. Varzi promised to do his best but was puzzled as to why Signor Rivio had flown all the way from Pisa to Tripoli to make such a basic request. Then Rivio put all his cards on the table: if Varzi won, he could have half of the lottery prize money. Moreover Rivio produced a document to that effect, drawn up by his solicitor. Varzi apparently made no firm promises, but as soon as his unexpected guest had departed, he is said to have telephoned his old adversary but new-found friend, Tazio Nuvolari.

Race day saw temperatures of over 100 degrees in the shade. The new circuit was described as running like a white ribbon between the palm trees and the yellow sand. The grandstand was resplendent with a mixture of Italian officers and Arab sheikhs while nearby, in a special box, sat the 30 people from all walks of life, clutching the slip of paper which could prove their passport to riches. There was a Milan butcher, an old lady from Florence, a student, a baron who had fallen on hard times ... and there was Signor Rivio, his bald pate beaded with perspiration, his face ruddy from a combination of the heat and the anticipation.

In a display of pomp and ceremony, Marshal Balbo flagged away the 30 starters, but instead of the expected Italian domination, it was Birkin's privately entered green Maserati who led them round followed by Nuvolari (Alfa), Giuseppe Campari (Maserati) and Varzi's Bugatti. On lap five of 30, Campari took the lead and Nuvolari also got past Birkin. At that stage Varzi was already 57 seconds behind the leader. Signor Rivio was observed mopping his brow. By lap 12 Campari was nine seconds ahead of Nuvolari, with Baconin Borzacchini up to third and Birkin hanging on gamely in fourth. Varzi appeared to be making little impact.

On lap 14 Campari came into the pits to refuel, allowing Nuvolari into the lead. Then Campari had to stop again because the Maserati's oil tank had worked itself loose. He lost 15 minutes while the tank was bound tight with rope and, although he rejoined the race, he dropped out shortly afterwards. He was soon spotted drowning his sorrows with a bottle of Chianti. Meanwhile from second place, Birkin had come in to refuel on lap 16. Maserati had sent only one mechanic to service both Birkin's car and Campari's and since the Englishman was a private entry, Campari took precedence and commandeered the mechanic. This left Birkin to enlist the services of a local garageman, who was such a drunk that he spent the entire race asleep under a palm tree. Heroically performing his own pitwork, Birkin lost two places through the prolonged stop, dropping down to fourth.

At two-thirds distance, Nuvolari's lead had been greatly reduced by Borzacchini with Louis Chiron not far behind in third. Then Varzi made his move, and by lap 25 he was up to third as Chiron and Birkin started to falter. The Bugatti was making ominous noises, however. Two cylinders were dead and the car was slowing. To stop for a change of plugs would have seen the end of any realistic chance he had of winning the race. Signor Rivio must have been about to tear up his ticket, especially with Nuvolari seemingly on the brink of lapping Varzi.

Until now, everything on the track had appeared above board, but the closing laps were decidedly irregular. First, on lap 27, Borzacchini inexplicably slowed and kept looking over his shoulder. Then he cut a corner so fine that he hit one of the empty oil drum markers. The car skidded to a halt with a burst tyre. Borzacchini was out of the race, but appeared none too concerned. Nuvolari began the last lap 30 seconds ahead of Varzi, but with half a mile (0.8km) remaining the Mantuan, too, began looking anxiously over his shoulder. The Alfa slowed alarmingly until, just 100 yards (91.4m) from the finish, it ground to a halt. Nuvolari jumped out and screamed: 'No petrol! No petrol!' Mechanics rushed to his assistance, but the delay allowed the ailing Varzi to loom into view. Nuvolari suddenly got going again but not in time to prevent Varzi crossing the line, almost in slow motion, the winner by one-tenth of a second. Exhausted, Varzi was carried shoulder-high by the crowds. Among the first to congratulate him was Signor Rivio. That evening, as Varzi, Nuvolari and Borzacchini sipped the finest champagne, rumours began to circulate that the race had been fixed. These three were named as the prime suspects with Campari and Chiron also suspected of being fringe players. At a hastily convened meeting of the country's supreme sporting authority the following morning, there were calls for all five to be disqualified and for their competition licences to be withdrawn. The demand was rejected. To have thrown out five of the most famous drivers in Europe might have dealt a fatal blow to the image of motor racing. Instead they escaped with a mild warning. However, in future the lottery system was changed so that ticket numbers were drawn just five minutes before the race when the drivers were already in their cars and were therefore immune to temptation.

If Borzacchini and Campari did profit from the race, they did not enjoy their good fortune for long. Four months later both were killed at the Monza Grand Prix when their cars hit an oil patch dropped by Count Trossi's Duesenberg on the South Curve.

The controversial Tripoli Grand Prix was also to prove Birkin's last race. In finishing an honourable third, he had reached out of the Maserati for a cigarette and had burned his arm on the hot exhaust pipe. He paid no attention to the burns until they flared up a few weeks later. Blood poisoning set in and he died on 22 June.

LE MANS VICTORY
SEALED BY CHEWING GUM

LE MANS 24-HOUR RACE,
17 JUNE 1933

More than a few eyebrows were raised when Alfa Romeo announced its pairings for the 1933 Le Mans Endurance Race. Raymond Sommer and Tazio Nuvolari in the same team? Neither was exactly fond of playing a supporting role. What were Alfa thinking of?

The Frenchman had won the previous year's race in partnership with Luigi Chinetti, but had insisted on driving 20 of the 24 hours himself as he had infinitely more confidence in his own ability than that of his co-driver. Chinetti was probably not in a position to argue too much with this high-handed approach, but Nuvolari was a different matter altogether. He would not act as anyone's chauffeur. The potential clash of egos was frightening.

True to form, Sommer loftily declared that he would be doing most of the driving in 1933 since Nuvolari was not as familiar with Le Mans as he was, and anyway the Italian was a known car-wrecker. If Nuvolari was allowed to remain at the wheel for more than a few hours, he would be sure to blow the Alfa's engine. No, the only hope of success was for Sommer to take the lion's share. For once, Nuvolari exercised considerable restraint, pointing out politely but firmly that he was a leading Grand Prix driver who knew his way round every circuit in the world and would not be troubled by a simple configuration such as Le Mans. Sommer backed down and, albeit reluctantly, agreed that they should divide the driving equally. In the end this unlikely arrangement worked, but for all the merging of two great talents, it was a simple piece of chewing gum that won the day.

Sommer and Nuvolari's short-wheelbase Mille Miglia type Alfa was one of 29 starters. Others included a noisy 6.8-litre V8 Duesenberg, entered by Prince Nicholas of Romania. The American car was popular with European royalty, but was too cumbersome for Le Mans where its high fuel consumption led to its downfall, it being disqualified after just 22 laps for refuelling sooner than was permitted.

Sommer took first turn in the favourites' car and got away to a good start, leading at the end of the first lap from the fellow Alfas of Louis Chiron and Franco Cortese, Chinetti and Varent, and the English duo of Brian Lewis and Tim Rose-Richards. By 24 laps Sommer had established a healthy advantage, at which point he was persuaded to hand over to Nuvolari. Contrary to fears, Nuvolari did not break the car and when he handed it back to Sommer that night, they had a lead of more than two laps over Chinetti and Varent. Everything seemed to be going smoothly until half-distance, when Sommer came in to the pits because the front wing had broken loose and the petrol tank had developed a leak through the constant vibration. Hasty repairs were carried out, the hole in the tank was plugged with chewing gum, and 15 minutes later Nuvolari rejoined the race, now over a lap behind the Chinetti/Varent car. Such a deficit was nothing to a man of Nuvolari's stature and over the next few hours he set about catching and eventually overhauling the lead car. By ten o'clock on the Sunday morning – when little more than half of the field were still running – Nuvolari and Sommer led by a lap. This position was strengthened by the departure of Cortese, who rolled his car out of the race at the Esses.

Until now the chewing gum had done its job admirably, but suddenly the makeshift fuel tank repair gave way and

Sommer was forced to make another unscheduled pit stop. With no satisfactory means of sealing the leak, it was evident that more stops might be necessary and so, being the faster driver, Nuvolari took the wheel in the hope that he could minimise the effect of the frequent fuel stops. How Sommer reacted to this order is not documented.

With less than an hour to go Nuvolari was barely two minutes ahead of Chinetti, but then another wretched fuel stop allowed Chinetti to take the lead. It seemed that Nuvolari's valiant efforts would be in vain. With just one lap remaining Nuvolari moved up into a challenging position and swept past Chinetti. But the latter was not about to surrender and surprised Nuvolari by regaining the lead. Then at Arnage, Chinetti, under intense pressure, missed a gear change, allowing Nuvolari through once more and he held on to win by 400 yards (366m), the lead having changed hands three times in the final 8 miles (12.9km) of a classic 24-hour race.

Encouragingly for the British contingent, of the 13 finishers, they filled the next five places. Lewis and Rose-Richards were third, 287 miles (462km) ahead of a 1.1-litre Riley driven by Peacock and van der Becke. Aston Martins finished fifth and seventh, sandwiching a new 750cc MG.

But the day belonged to Nuvolari, who had broken the lap record no fewer than nine times. It is doubtful whether Sommer ever questioned the little Italian's driving skills again.

THE WRONG PIT SIGNAL
LE MANS 24-HOUR RACE,
15 JUNE 1935

Back in the 1930s the pit board was a driver's sole means of communication with his team. So when the Alfa team signalled to Frenchman René-Louis Dreyfus that he was comfortably leading the Le Mans 24-Hour Race in the closing stages, he eased off accordingly to preserve the car. Imagine his horror therefore when at 4p.m. as the cars crossed the finish line, Dreyfus discovered that his crew had blundered. Instead of winning, he was five minutes behind in second place and had missed the opportunity to close the gap. The Alfa camp would not have been a happy place that Sunday night.

There were 58 starters, 36 of them British, including six Rileys and seven Aston Martins. Alfa Romeo had won the previous four races but the team proved less reliable this year … and not only in terms of their pit signals. Nevertheless it was the four supercharged Alfas who set the early pace, the Brian Lewis/Earl Howe car leading for the first six laps before stopping for a change of distributor. The Luigi Chinetti/Gastard Alfa then took over but dropped back after the first hour, having been delayed by a wheel change. This opened the way for a third Alfa with the experienced Raymond Sommer at the wheel. Sommer was having to drive solo as his co-driver, de Sauge, had been conveniently taken ill! Sommer built up a lead of two laps but as a wet evening gave way to a wet night, he lost seven laps due to a blocked fuel line and eventually retired early on Sunday morning. At midnight there was a new leader – the 4.5-litre British Racing Green Lagonda driven by John Hindmarsh and Louis Fontes – but both the Lewis/Howe and Dreyfus/Stoffel Alfas were on the same lap, as was a 4.9-litre Bugatti.

The Alfas' tale of woe continued when the Chinetti/Gastard car retired after twice going off the road and Earl Howe's car broke a piston. This left just one Alfa running. Dreyfus and Stoffel lost valuable time, too, having their shock absorbers changed, and by midday on the Sunday appeared to have little chance of catching the Lagonda. A British victory to end the run of Italian domination seemed a foregone conclusion at the start of the final hour, only for the Lagonda to hit trouble. Fontes was forced to make several stops with fading oil pressure, allowing the Alfa to close right up. When Dreyfus passed the stricken Lagonda as it sat in its pit, the Alfa team signalled that he was now in the lead. In fact he was still a lap behind and, making no attempt to speed up, remained in that position at the chequered flag.

With a British victory and 22 of the 28 finishers being British, there was much celebration in the bars and cafés of Le Mans that night. But for Alfa, Italy and an unhappy French driver, it was the race that got away.

NUVOLARI
VERSUS THE GERMANS
GERMAN GRAND PRIX, 28 JULY 1935

By the summer of 1935 German nationalism was reaching its height. The self-styled master race could not countenance defeat in any shape or form – in the political arena, on the battlefield, or on the football pitch or running track. This sense of superiority applied equally to the motor racing circuit, where the sleek silver Mercedes and Auto-Unions were sweeping all before them. Germany not only had the fastest cars, but also the finest drivers – men like Rudolf Caracciola, Manfred von Brauchitsch and Bernd Rosemeyer, the new sensation who, like so many of his predecessors, had risen from the ranks of motorcycling. In their spotless white overalls, the Germans appeared clinical and efficient, and their public came to view them as unbeatable.

The march to power had begun in 1934 when, after Alfa Romeo victories in Monaco and France, Mercedes and Auto-Union had carved up the rest of the season between them, notching wins in Germany, Switzerland, Italy, Spain and Czechoslovakia. They carried on the good work in 1935. Luigi Fagioli won the Monaco Grand Prix for Mercedes; Achille Varzi (Auto-Union) triumphed in Tunis; and Caracciola's Mercedes won in Tripoli, France and Belgium. Nothing was expected to stand in the way of the silver machines on home soil, and a regiment of dedicated Nazis marched 350 miles (563km) to the Nürburgring in anticipation of another German clean sweep. The line-up was headed by five Mercedes (Caracciola, Fagioli, von Brauchitsch, Hermann Lang and Hans Geier) and four Auto-Unions (Rosemeyer, Achille Varzi, Hans Stuck and Paul Pietsch). The best the Italians could muster by way of competition were three Alfa Romeo P3s, driven by Tazio Nuvolari, Louis Chiron and Antonio Brivio. But even on a circuit with 176 corners, the Alfas' 265bhp would surely be no match for the Auto-Unions' 350bhp and the Mercedes' 400bhp.

Despite the drivers' preference for starting positions on the grid to be decided by practice times, the organisers insisted on a ballot, which put the crowd favourite, Caracciola, back on the fourth row. Any spectator apprehension was quashed immediately when Caracciola, shooting off almost before the flag had fallen, stormed straight into the lead. Fagioli lay second but before the end of the first of the 22 laps had surrendered that position to the slender figure of Nuvolari who, in his familiar uniform of sky blue trousers and yellow sweater, had steered the Alfa around the outside of the pack in a daring manoeuvre. At the end of that opening lap, Caracciola sped past the pits at 170mph (273.6km/h), followed 12 seconds later by Nuvolari who clocked 150mph (241.4km/h), and Fagioli close up in third. On the second lap it was Rosemeyer's turn to force his way through the field, relegating Nuvolari to fifth behind Caracciola, Rosemeyer, Fagioli and von Brauchitsch. Soon Chiron passed Nuvolari and moved up to fourth when Rosemeyer had to stop for a wheel change. But by lap five both Chiron and Brivio had retired, with transmission trouble and a broken differential respectively, leaving Nuvolari alone against the might of the Germans.

The situation certainly seemed to appeal to the little Italian, who took the fight to the Germans in inspirational fashion. By oversteering round each corner in a four-wheel drift (a technique which he pioneered), Nuvolari was able to gain precious seconds and work his way back up through the field. By lap ten only Caracciola remained ahead, but even he could not hold off the irresistible Nuvolari who, to the horror of the German crowd, swept past him into the lead. Then came the high drama of the race. At the end of the eleventh lap – half-distance – the leading five cars came into the pits to refuel and change wheels. Von Brauchitsch got away in 47 seconds but in the Alfa pit a pumping device broke and, amid much panic, the refuelling operation had to be completed by hand with a funnel. Excitable at the best of times, Nuvolari went spare and, in his frustration, downed an entire bottle of mineral water, pausing only to swear at his hapless mechanics. The stop took a calamitous 2min 14sec and when he eventually rejoined the race, Nuvolari had fallen back to sixth. It was nothing short of a disaster.

The efforts of von Brauchitsch's pit crew had hoisted him into the lead from Caracciola, Rosemeyer and Fagioli, but Nuvolari quickly began to make up some of the lost ground and in the course of one lap – the thirteenth – he passed Stuck, Fagioli, Caracciola and Rosemeyer to rise to second place, just 69 seconds in arrears. Von Brauchitsch responded by setting a new lap record of 10min 30sec and by 14 laps had increased his advantage to 1min 26sec. He then appeared to ease off in the belief that victory was a foregone conclusion, and this enabled Nuvolari to make renewed inroads into the lead, cutting it back lap by lap – to 63 seconds, then 47, 43 and, starting the final circuit, 35. Such a lead should still have been sufficient for the German to take the chequered flag in first place, but as he passed the pits he could be seen pointing frantically at his left-side rear tyre. The same tyre had begun to show alarming signs of wear at the start of the previous lap, but Mercedes team boss Alfred Neubauer had overridden his mechanics' pleas to bring von Brauchitsch in for a tyre change. 'Brauchitsch will make it,' he snapped, 'and so will the tyre. It's only a question of a few minutes.' The tyre didn't make it.

Coming out of a corner less than 6 miles (9.7km) from the finish, the Mercedes' tyre collapsed. Von Brauchitsch skilfully managed to retain control but could do nothing more than grind home slowly on the rim. Nuvolari swept past imperiously to win what the world's press described as 'a historic triumph of man over machine'. Stuck was nearly two minutes behind in second with Caracciola, who later complained of having felt unwell during the race, third, Rosemeyer fourth and von Brauchitsch fifth.

The 250,000-strong crowd were stunned by this blow to German supremacy. The loudspeakers, which had been prepared to announce another German victory, remained ominously silent. The organisers eventually conducted a search for the Italian flag, which was then half-heartedly raised but without the accompaniment of the Italian national anthem, for the simple reason that nobody had bothered to bring the record. Except Nuvolari, that is. He always carried a record of the anthem in his suitcase for good luck, so he sent his mechanic to fetch it and the spectators were finally able to listen to the least popular tune in Germany that afternoon. It must have been a bitter pill to swallow, but for Nuvolari it was probably his finest hour. One of motor racing's strangest races was also one of its greatest.

AN ENCOUNTER WITH A STAG

DONINGTON GRAND PRIX, 22 OCTOBER 1938

In an era when motor racing had a disturbingly high mortality rate, most drivers regarded serious injury – or worse – as an occupational hazard. But few treated it in quite as cavalier a fashion as Tazio Nuvolari. From the moment he first arrived on the scene on two wheels back in the 1920s, the Italian ace had made it clear that in the event of a pre-race accident, only a formal death certificate was likely to prevent him competing. Doctors despaired of him. A crash in the 1925 Italian Grand Prix at Monza put him in hospital, where he was swathed in bandages like an Egyptian mummy. Yet seven days later he took part in a motorcycle race, having persuaded medics to bandage him in such a manner that he could be placed on his machine in a riding posture.

Having moved up to four wheels on a regular basis, he broke a leg at Alessandria in 1934 when his Maserati skidded into a tree on the wet road. After four weeks in hospital as the world's most impatient patient, Nuvolari defied the advice of the doctors and entered to drive a Maserati in the Avus Grand Prix in Germany. He had the pedals of the car specially adapted so that all three could be operated with one foot (the other still being in plaster), and before the race he was presented by a local gymnastic club with a chunk of the tree which he had hit in Alessandria. The inscription read: 'To Tazio Nuvolari, intrepid ace of the wheel, as a record of the providential obstacle which though preventing a sure victory saved a precious existence.' The sight of him hobbling out on crutches for practice sessions and having to be helped in and out of the cockpit must have done wonders for his opponents' confidence but, despite being plagued by cramp, he managed to finish a gallant fifth. The fourth-placed Earl Howe said of Nuvolari's drive: 'Let any who say it was foolhardy at least be honest and admit it was one of the finest exhibitions of pluck and grit ever seen. By such men are victories won!'

Two years later, while Nuvolari was practising for the Tripoli Grand Prix, a wheel of his Alfa Romeo caught a marker stone at over 125mph (201.2km/h). The tyre burst, the car turned over and ended up in the sand which bordered the circuit. For his part, Nuvolari was flung into the air like a doll and landed in a heap of parched grass. Helpers who rushed to the scene found the smoking car but no sign of its driver until, ten minutes later, the stricken Nuvolari was located deep in the grass, lying unconscious with damaged ribs and severe bruising. In hospital he was put into plaster and ordered to rest for several days. 'But of course,' came the reply. 'After the race I shall do so!' The next day, although scarcely able to move in his plaster corset, he drove a replacement Alfa into seventh place. It was the stuff of which legends are made.

The Donington Grand Prix had first attracted the mighty German teams in 1937 and had proved such a success (Bernd Rosemeyer winning in an Auto-Union) that they returned in force to the tree-lined Leicestershire circuit for the 1938 race. It was scheduled to be the last major event of the season, listed for 2 October, but when the German teams arrived a week earlier to start practice, they found themselves slap in the middle of the Munich crisis. In case war was about to break out, the Germans hurried home and the race was cancelled, but once Chamberlain had returned with his promise of 'peace for our time', the contest was rearranged for 22 October and the Germans returned.

Three days before the race the 45-year-old Nuvolari took his Auto-Union out for a practice session. That he was now at the wheel of a German car was the result of a considerable fall-out with his Italian employers. He was approximately halfway round the circuit when a huge stag emerged from some woods and ran straight across the track, ploughing into Nuvolari's car. Nuvolari stopped 200 yards (183m) further on and limped back to attend to the animal which was lying in a pool of blood. Back at the pits ambulance men were worried by Nuvolari's non-appearance and so they drove off to search for him. They found him stroking the dead stag. 'You cannot take anyone to the hospital,' he said gravely, 'not even this unfortunate one. He died on the spot.' In fact Nuvolari was in need of hospital treatment, having fractured a rib in the collision, but he no longer wanted to be bothered with doctors and nurses. He was not prepared to risk being told he could not drive in the race. Instead he asked for the stag to be taken away and prepared himself for the race. After persuading the organisers to agree to his request to have the stag's head stuffed and mounted, he got out his lucky corset, which he had improvised for himself using tight bandages, and set out to thrill the British public in the same way that he had captivated spectators all over mainland Europe.

In the absence of Rudolf Caracciola, who had burnt his foot during the Italian Grand Prix and in any case was said not to like Donington as a circuit, Hermann Lang took pole in a Mercedes from Nuvolari, Manfred von Brauchitsch in a second Mercedes and the great British hope, Richard Seaman, in a third. Near the back of the grid was an ERA driven by band-leader Billy Cotton. A crowd of 60,000 turned up to watch the Duke of Kent start the 80-lap race with a Union Jack. From the off, Nuvolari shot into the lead from his Auto-Union team-mate Hermann Müller and the

Mercedes trio of von Brauchitsch, Seaman and Lang, and stayed at the head of affairs until lap 20 when he went into the pits for a change of plugs. Emerging in fourth spot behind Müller, Seaman and Lang, Nuvolari was about to lap Hanson's Alta when the tail-ender dropped a sump full of oil on the descent to the hairpin. Nuvolari picked his way through the hazard but Seaman was not as fortunate and spun off the road, promoting Nuvolari to third. He was still third after the mid-race refuelling stops but Lang had now taken over pole position from Müller. Driving with typical verve and flair and, according to contemporary reports, a huge grin on his face, Nuvolari proceeded to reel in the front two. He passed Müller and on lap 67 overtook Lang for a lead he was never to relinquish. Showing no ill effects from his severely restricted movement, he pulled away to win by 32 seconds from Lang, Seaman, Müller and von Brauchitsch.

Nuvolari received a rapturous welcome from all except some of the serious punters in the bookmakers' enclosure. They had torn up their tickets when he had looked to be out of the race following his practice accident and now they were furious with themselves. Two days after crossing the finish line the 'Maestro', as he was known, was presented with the Grand Prix trophy along with the mounted stag's head, which he intended to take with him to other tracks as a lucky mascot. It would be another 16 years before a German Grand Prix car would again race on English soil, but in the meantime Nuvolari's epic drive under unbelievably difficult circumstances would provide a lasting memory through the dark days of the Second World War.

THE TIED MONTE
MONTE CARLO RALLY, JANUARY 1939

The 1938 Monte Carlo Rally had seen the introduction of a mountain section through the French Alps, thereby providing an exacting new test and further establishing the event as an all-round examination of driving skills. In particular the ascent and descent of the treacherous Col des Leques had proved such an attraction that the Alpine route from Grenoble was retained for the following year. The Alpine route was divided into five sections and had a target average speed of 31mph (49.9km/h). The first section went from Grenoble over the Col de la Croix Haute to St Julien en Bouchène, where the relatively straightforward second section began. Section three was short and sharp – an 8 mile (12.9km) sprint from Barrème to Castellane via the twisty, and invariably icy, Col des Leques. Section four from Castellane to Grasse took the drivers over the Col de Luens, and finally section five was the run through Nice to Monte Carlo.

For 1939, a total of 500 bonus points were awarded to starters from Athens, 498 points from Bucharest or Tallinn, 497 from Stavanger or Palermo, and 496 from John O'Groats or Umea. With every point vital in the final reckoning, 42 of the 121 starters chose Athens, although aviator Amy Johnson was one of 24 setting out from John O'Groats. While the Scandinavian routes were badly hit by snow, a series of landslides near Salonika were cleared in time for the Athens starters to get through. The conditions on the Alps were less severe than had been anticipated – even the Col des Leques was clear – with the result that the majority of the competitors were able to keep within the time limits and not incur penalty points. Since the Alpine route had failed to thin out the field, everything rested on the final two sections – the driving test and the speed hill climb, the latter a new feature for that year. The driving test consisted of a 200 yard (183m) sprint, a fast reverse over a line, and then another 100 yard (91.4m) dash to the finish.

The joint leaders going into the test were Jean Trevoux and co-driver M. Lesurque (the 1938 runners-up) in a 3.5-litre Hotchkiss, and Jean Paul and co-driver M. Contet in a 3.5-litre Delahaye. Both had started from Athens and both had been unpenalised between Grenoble and Monte Carlo. Moreover, they recorded the same time – 25.8 seconds – for the driving test. They were actually beaten in the driving test by the 1938 winner Bakker Schut in a Ford V8, but he had started from Tallinn where there were fewer bonus points to be earned. So this left Trevoux and Paul still tied for the lead with just the corkscrew hill climb at Eze remaining. Incredibly, they again recorded identical times – 72.6 seconds – in being the fastest up the hill, and so for the first and only time in the history of the Monte Carlo Rally, the event ended in a tie.

THE WRONG SIDE
OF THE ROAD

GRAN PREMIO
INTERNACIONAL DEL NORTE,
27 SEPTEMBER 1940

This South American marathon produced one of the first major victories in the glorious career of Juan Manuel Fangio, but it so nearly ended in disaster following a horrendous blunder by his mechanic who, disorientated by being in a strange country, forgot which side of the road he was supposed to be driving on and smashed into a private car.

In 1939 the Argentine Automobile Club started work on an ambitious project to link Buenos Aires and New York by road. Hoping that road racing might persuade the relevant authorities to construct a network of paved roads through South America, the AAC conceived the Gran Premio Internacional del Norte, a 5,868 mile (9,443km) race to be run over 13 stages, starting and finishing in Buenos Aires and taking the competitors as far north as the Peruvian city of Lima. Precious little of the route was paved – only the first 400 miles (644km) or so to Cordoba – much of the journey through Peru being on mountainous dirt tracks with alarming drops to one, or sometimes both, sides. The climb across the Andes reached altitudes of over 13,000ft (3,962m) – a daunting prospect for drivers who were not equipped with such essential items as oxygen cylinders. It was to be a tremendous test of stamina and driving skill, the sole respite being a two-day break at Lima.

The 29-year-old Fangio was just starting out in motor sport. Driving a Chevrolet coupé, he faced stiff opposition from brothers Oscar and Juan Gálvez; Ernesto Blanco, Argentine champion driver of 1936; and Angel Lo Valvo, the 1939 Argentine champion. Familiarising himself with the route before the actual race, Fangio recalled pulling into a remote Bolivian village for the night and asking for the toilet. He was somewhat taken aback to be shown to a patch of waste ground where a pig was rooting around. That was public convenience, Bolivian style.

The race started at one minute past midnight from the stadium of River Plate Football Club, the starting order having been determined by drawing lots. The first stage – between Buenos Aires and the Argentine town of Tucuman – covered 847 miles (1,363km), a stage distance never before attempted in that type of racing. Enrique Valiente (who drove under the name of 'Patoruzu') led on the initial stretch to Rosario but by Cordoba, the Gálvez brothers had taken over, chased by Boris Afanacenco, Pedro Cavacevich and Fangio. Slowly but surely, Fangio's reconnaissance trip began to pay off and at the end of that long first stage he found himself in the lead. The Gálvez brothers won the second and third stages (to La Quiaca and Potosi respectively), a number of the crews being affected by the altitude on the plains of Bolivia. Among the casualties was Lo Valvo, who had to return from La Quiaca to his native Arrecife when his co-driver and brother-in-law, Antonio Spampinatto, was taken ill as a result of a lack of oxygen. With only one doctor competing in the race, there was little chance of medical attention en route.

Having arrived safely in La Paz at the end of the fourth stage, Fangio was nearly put out of the race through no fault of his own. His mechanic, Héctor Tieri, went to fetch the Chevrolet but forgot that whereas in Argentina they drove on the left, in Bolivia they drove on the right. Setting off on the wrong side of the road, he ploughed straight into another car. The accident left the Chevrolet with a bent chassis and a twisted axle and necessitated hasty repairs before it could set off on the next stage.

Then on the way to Lima a fan blade broke and made a hole in the radiator. The gap was plugged with a handkerchief and a piece of rag, and Fangio continued on his way. The delay meant that he was only eleventh on that stage, but he still led overall.

On the return from Lima, the Gálvez brothers went off the road at night, Oscar breaking his shoulder-blade and he and Juan finishing up at the bottom of a ravine with the Ford coupé. Julio Pérez went off at the same corner, leaving his car balancing precariously on the edge of the precipice. Hearing cries, he shone his spotlight into the dark depths of the ravine and located the Gálvez brothers!

The elimination of his closest rivals left Fangio with a lead of some 90 minutes and although he contrived to hit a large rock on the penultimate stage between La Quiaca and Tucuman, he ended up winning as comfortably as anyone could in a race where he never quite knew what was around the next corner and where his mechanic couldn't be trusted to drive more than 100 yards.

RACING ON ICE
SWEDISH WINTER GRAND PRIX,
22 FEBRUARY 1947

Motor racing on ice had been a popular spectator sport in Scandinavia since 1931, when the first Swedish Winter Grand Prix was run on the frozen Lake Rämen. Among the entrants that year was German ace Rudolf Caracciola, but he was unable to master the surface as expertly as the Finnish drivers. For the following year's event a crowd of 60,000 turned up. Lake Vallentuna, north of Stockholm, became a regular venue of ice races from 1934 and it was there, 13 years later, that Reg Parnell and the ERA team swept all before them in the first post-war Swedish Winter Grand Prix.

Manufactured between 1935 and 1939, the ERAs (it stood for English Racing Automobiles) raced with some distinction either side of the war even though only 17 were ever made. Three fell into the hands of Reg Parnell, George Abecassis and Leslie Brooke, who took them to Sweden for the Grand Prix at Rommehed on 9 February 1947. The race turned into an ERA walkover because their chief rivals – the French – were stranded miles away on a ship stuck fast in ice. So it was decided to rerun the event 13 days later on Lake Vallentuna, by which time the French challenge was expected to materialise. Indeed it did, led by Raymond Sommer, but he proved no match for the wily Parnell.

Between the two races Parnell had to arrange for spare parts to be sent over from England after his engine had blown.

He also had the idea of fitting twin rear wheels to the ERA to improve its road-holding on the ice of Lake Vallentuna. As a frequent competitor in hill climbs, he owned a set of extra-long hubs to facilitate the fitting of twin wheels, but unfortunately they were at home in England, and he was in Sweden. So he phoned his nephew and instructed him to get the hubs and a spare set of wheels to London Airport and over to Gothenburg that night. When Parnell fitted them to the ERA, Sommer immediately objected but the Englishman had checked the rules beforehand and had found that there was nothing to preclude twin rear wheels.

The race began in temperatures of minus 15 degrees Fahrenheit, most of the drivers wearing RAF flying jackets to keep out the cold. A 3½ mile (5.6km) circuit had been snowploughed across the lake, the surface of which was sheet ice. Since nobody was permitted to use studded tyres, the organisers had spread fine gravel over the entire course and then sprayed it with water to give it a texture like sandpaper. This certainly improved the grip, but it was Parnell's extra rear wheels which really made the difference. No car could match the road-holding of his ERA and he skated to victory at an average speed of 68⅙mph (109.7km/h) – a triumph of British ingenuity.

THE SILVERSTONE SHEEP
MUTTON GRAND PRIX, SEPTEMBER 1947

It is a sobering thought that Silverstone may never have become the venue for the British Grand Prix but for an animated drinking session in a Worcestershire public house. Fresh from a satisfactory day's competition at the nearby Shelsley Walsh hill climb, a group of drivers were in good spirits at the Mitre Oak, Ombersley, one evening in September 1947 and were discussing where they might be able to race next. Their options appeared strictly limited, Brooklands having been sold and Donington Park still being cluttered with military vehicles. Then one of their number, an enthusiast by the name of Maurice Geoghegan, happened to mention a virtually disused airfield near his home village of Silverstone in Northamptonshire. He said that he had tested a Frazer Nash on the airfield the previous year and had mapped out a perfectly satisfactory 2 mile (3.2km) circuit along the perimeter roads and one of the runways. Why didn't they go the next day?

After drinking to what was clearly an excellent idea, the owners of 11 Frazer Nashes and a Bugatti set off for Silverstone the following morning, where they were joined, so the story goes, by the pilot of a passing Tiger Moth who landed on the runway and tried his luck at the wheel of one of the cars. During practice one driver ran over an old garden fork, the impact causing the implement to spring up and stab him in the arm. Although there were reportedly no fewer than four doctors present, none bothered to attend the wound, which finally stopped bleeding of its own accord.

Precious few details are known about the race itself other than that Geoghegan was on the approach to Stowe when his Frazer Nash hit an errant sheep. It was the end of the road for both car and sheep, the latter receiving the scant consolation that the race would be known thereafter as the Mutton Grand Prix. The meeting finished in the time-honoured tradition – at the Saracen's Head, Towcester.

Word got around. Within a year of Geoghegan's pioneering race, Silverstone airfield was staging its first British Grand Prix. Then in 1949 it adopted the familiar perimeter-only layout which remained in use for many years and helped establish Silverstone as the home of British motor racing.

FARINA IN A HUFF

ITALIAN GRAND PRIX,
11 SEPTEMBER 1949

The usual practice among teams running three or four cars in a race when the drivers were evenly matched was to allow them to sort out the placings for themselves over the opening laps and then to signal to them to maintain those positions for the duration. No team wanted its drivers cutting each other's throats by risking needless overtaking manoeuvres, so it made sense to have an arranged finishing order. And it was equally desirable for the drivers to play some part in reaching that decision. Alfa Romeo, however, had its own ideas. Alfa insisted on picking the winner itself and often signalled the leading Alfa driver to slow down so that a team-mate could overtake him. Not surprisingly, this policy did not always go down well with the drivers.

The first signs of rebellion occurred at the 1946 Turin Grand Prix when the Frenchman Jean-Pierre Wimille was instructed by the Alfa pit to ease off and allow team-mate Achille Varzi through to win. This resulted in a huge post-race row, as a result of which Wimille was dropped from the Alfa team for the forthcoming Milan Grand Prix, an event which was run over two heats and a final. Alfa driver Giuseppe 'Nino' Farina, an Italian doctor of engineering, finished first in his heat but was subsequently relegated to third for jumping the start. As far as Farina was concerned his moral victory in the heat had earned him the right to be allowed to win the final, but instead Alfa announced that Count Felice

Trossi was to be given preferential treatment. Obeying team orders, Varzi let Trossi through to the front after a few laps. Farina was now close up in third, but there was no way that Varzi was going to give way this time. Instead the pair were locked in a ferocious duel with Varzi seemingly desperate to prevent Farina from going after Trossi. Eventually the battle took its toll and Farina's brakes started to give him trouble. When he spun at a corner, instead of rejoining the race in third place, he simply retired in a huff because he hadn't been permitted to win. That evening at a local café, his behaviour was described as 'aloof and sulky'.

In the wake of his temper tantrum at Milan, Farina was told that his services were no longer required by Alfa. He did not compete anywhere in 1947, raising speculation that he had retired, but he was back in 1948, and the following year's Italian Grand Prix at Monza found him at the wheel of one of the new Maseratis. The race was eagerly anticipated in Italian circles since it marked the Grand Prix debut of Ferrari and was expected to herald the return to competitive action of Alfa Romeo. The Alfa presence failed to materialise, however, leaving the Ferrari boys to have matters pretty much their own way. Although running in third place, Farina soon realised that his Maserati was no match for the two leading Ferraris. The further into the distance they disappeared, the more despondent he became until finally he once again dropped out for no obvious reason. There was nothing mechanically wrong with his car – he had just given up because he was unable to catch the Ferraris. One of these subsequently retired, meaning that Farina could have finished second, but he was never interested in being second best. Alberto Ascari went on to gain a comfortable victory in his Ferrari from Philippe Etancelin's French Talbot and the Maserati driven by Prince Bira of Siam. Piero Taruffi in the other works Maserati struggled on to finish seventh, 16 laps behind the winner. Farina could not be bothered.

Ironically, following the deaths of Varzi and Wimille in crashes and Trossi from cancer, Farina was given another chance by Alfa in 1950 and went on to win the inaugural World Drivers' Championship. For once he was happy.

CALLED FROM THE BAR

LE MANS 24-HOUR RACE,
13 JUNE 1953

The preparation for an endurance race such as Le Mans is all-important. Drivers need to be at the peak of physical fitness with a clear head and razor-sharp reactions. What they do not need is a hangover, which is why the triumphant 1953 drive of Tony Rolt and Duncan Hamilton has entered Jaguar folklore. Following the 1952 débâcle at Le Mans, Jaguar was anxious to make amends the following year. And this time it boasted an innovation which worked – disc brakes. The inclusion of these at the expense of the traditional drum gave the Jaguar drivers a crucial advantage, allowing them to brake later into corners. The team, which had won in 1951 with Peter Walker and Peter Whitehead, entered three works C-types – to be driven by Walker and Stirling Moss, Whitehead and Jimmy Stewart, and, as reserves, Rolt and Hamilton. The last-named pair would only be able to race if one of the 60 accepted starters dropped out beforehand. Rolt and Hamilton waited more in hope than expectation but by the Friday evening nobody had withdrawn. They were duly informed that their services would not be required.

So they did what most sportsmen would have done in such circumstances – they went out and got drunk ... very drunk. Rolt, a former army officer, and Hamilton, an ex-fighter pilot and generally larger-than-life character, drowned their sorrows with a vengeance, and by the early hours of Saturday morning they were suitably mellow. It was then that Jaguar team manager 'Lofty' England finally caught up with them, sitting on a pavement, and informed them that a team had made a late withdrawal from the 24-Hour Race. They were in the race after all. The news that in just over 12 hours' time they would be haring around Le Mans at 100mph (160.9km/h) should have had an instant sobering effect, but so much alcohol had been consumed that they were still feeling decidedly the worse for wear on the Saturday afternoon. Neither relished the prospect of taking the first stint at the wheel so they tossed a coin to decide who would *not* start. Rolt lost the toss.

Fortunately the fresh air soon cleared their hangovers and after an hour Rolt found himself in third place behind Moss/Walker and the Ferrari 375MM of Luigi Villoresi and Alberto Ascari. During the second hour Moss made two stops to clear a blocked fuel pipe, thereby dropping to twenty-first and allowing Villoresi to take the lead. But Rolt responded to the challenge by passing the Ferrari and setting a new lap record at 4min 30sec (115mph/185.1km/h), over ten seconds faster than Ascari had gone the previous year. Ascari's reply was equally emphatic, lowering the lap record to 4min 27.4sec and instigating a battle with the Jaguar which would last right through the night. But the Jaguar's superior braking always gave it the upper hand and by dawn on Sunday it had a two-lap advantage. After both cars had made routine stops around 8.30a.m., the Ferrari was heard to have a slipping clutch. Within two hours it had retired, leaving the way clear for Rolt and Hamilton to proceed to an unlikely win.

Although tired following their Friday night excesses, they managed to drive 2,540 miles (4,088km) at an average speed of 105⅞mph (170.3km/h) – the first time a Le Mans winner's speed had topped 100mph (160.9km/h). In fact the first seven cars home all averaged over 100mph. Moss and Walker fought their way back up the field to finish second, with Whitehead and Stewart fourth behind a Chrysler-engined 5.5-litre Cunningham.

As the Jaguar team toasted its success, two of its number were observed celebrating rather more gingerly than usual.

HELL IN BUENOS AIRES

ARGENTINE GRAND PRIX,
16 JANUARY 1955

With echoes of the energy-sapping 1926 European Grand Prix, this race was run in unbearably hot conditions. At the start of the three-hour ordeal, the temperature in the shade at Buenos Aires stood at 100 degrees Fahrenheit while ground temperatures exceeded a staggering 125 degrees. Only the strong or the acclimatised could hope to survive and in the event only two drivers – Juan Manuel Fangio and Roberto Mieres – were able to last the distance. Not surprisingly, both were Argentinians. Everyone else either gave up altogether or had to stop at some point for a rest, enabling a fresher driver to take over, so that in the course of the 96-lap race there were 16 driver substitutions among the 21 starters and more than 50 pit stops.

Froilan Gonzales put his Ferrari on pole, and back on the third row was up-and-coming British driver Stirling Moss, new to Mercedes-Benz for 1955, having been with Maserati. There was a typically mad rush into the first bend and when things sorted themselves out at the end of the opening lap Fangio's Mercedes had a slender advantage over Alberto Ascari (Lancia), Moss, Gonzales and Nino Farina (Ferrari). On the second lap a multiple crash involving Jean Behra and Karl Kling reduced the number of participants to 16, and on the following lap Ascari moved to the front, only to be overtaken soon after by Gonzales. The battle between Ascari and Gonzales raged until lap 22, when Ascari spun on a patch of oil and crashed into the fence.

As early as quarter-distance, drivers were coming into the pits in a state of extreme fatigue. After Ascari's retirement, Gonzales stopped for a rest, his car being taken over by Farina who himself had been relieved a matter of a few laps earlier by the Ferrari spare driver, Umberto Maglioli. When Farina soon found the going too tough, he was replaced for a time by Maurice Trintignant who, in a distinction shared with Behra, would go on to drive three different cars in the race. Meanwhile Moss retired on lap 30, too exhausted to continue, and abandoned his Mercedes at the side of the track. Four laps later Fangio, the new leader, stopped for refreshment and the welcome opportunity to pour cold water over himself. The delay allowed Harry Schell's Maserati to seize the initiative but soon the American, too, was affected by the heat and was substituted by Behra. Mieres had a stint in front until he was kept in the pits for ten minutes with fuel pump problems.

It was so hot in the stands that halfway through the race all of the soft drinks supplies had run out, forcing parched spectators to buy wine bottles filled with tap water which were brought in by an emergency fleet of lorries from the surrounding area. An indication of the debilitating nature of the heat was that one Ferrari actually had five different drivers, the car standing idle in the pits for an entire lap because none of the drivers was fit enough to take the wheel. Finally it was Gonzales who, after a prolonged rest and an injection to alleviate back pain, climbed into the cockpit, earning the nickname of 'Cabezon' (the stubborn one) from his home crowd.

Gonzales resumed the struggle a considerable distance behind Fangio but began closing at the rate of five seconds per lap. Fangio was now on the brink of collapse himself and on more than one occasion contemplated giving up. He later recalled: 'Once or twice I felt as if my Mercedes-Benz had caught fire. I turned right round to look, but there was nothing to be seen. It must have been the wind carrying the hot air from below the car, and up round the cockpit to burn my shoulder and neck.' A few laps from the finish Mercedes team boss Alfred Neubauer signalled to Fangio to come into the pits to hand over the car to Moss, who was now suitably refreshed by a shower, but Fangio pretended not to understand and pressed on. He kept going by imagining that he was lost in the snow. His predicament was helped by an accident to Gonzales who pressed so hard that he spun off, bending the Ferrari's front suspension. He was more than happy to hand the car back to Farina, who drove on to the finish. With one supreme last effort, Fangio came home almost two minutes ahead of the Gonzales/Farina/Trintignant/Gonzales/Farina Ferrari with the Farina/Maglioli/Trintignant/Maglioli Ferrari in third. When it came to the prize-giving, Fangio was so tired he could hardly stand. It had been that sort of a race.

HELPING HANDS

ITALIAN GRAND PRIX, 2 SEPTEMBER 1956

The 1956 Formula One World Drivers' Championship all boiled down to the last race of the season, at Monza. The destiny of the title lay between two men with hitherto contrasting careers – Juan Manuel Fangio, the brilliant Argentinian who had been world champion in each of the past two seasons, and Peter Collins, the young British driver who was just beginning to make his mark in Formula One. Fangio had won that year in Argentina, Britain and Germany, while Collins had triumphed in Belgium and France. Under the complicated points scoring system of the time, which took into account a driver's best five finishes, Fangio had 30 points from his best five. In order to add to his total, he had to finish first or second at the Italian Grand Prix. Going into that race, Collins had 22 points from four finishes. So if he were to win at Monza, set fastest lap (which earned an extra point) and Fangio were to finish outside the first two, Collins would snatch the title by 31 points to 30. There was everything to play for.

To complicate matters, Fangio and Collins were team-mates at Lancia-Ferrari. In the absence of Mercedes, who had withdrawn from Formula One in the wake of the 1955 Le Mans tragedy, Lancia-Ferrari had swept virtually all before them in 1956 and Monza looked like being no exception. Fangio took pole position from team-mates Eugenio Castellotti and Luigi Musso, but Collins could do no better than row three. Before the race Fangio had expressed concern about tyre wear, believing that it was the only thing which stood between his team and victory. He suggested to Castellotti and Musso that they carve up the race between them. Fangio offered to set the pace and then towards the finish, to allow the other two through to fight out victory. Fangio was perfectly content with third place so long as Collins wasn't in with a chance of winning. Fangio hoped that the idea of tucking in behind him and thereby conserving their tyres for much of the race would appeal to the two Italians but they wanted no part of it, preferring to go their own way.

As the flag fell, Fangio moved smoothly into the lead but was passed almost immediately by Musso and Castellotti, who seemed to be treating the race as one of five laps rather than 50. Their pace was suicidal and after just five laps, exactly as Fangio had predicted, both dived into the pits with their tyres in shreds, leaving the front four as Fangio, Stirling Moss in a Maserati 250F, Collins, and Harry Schell in a Vanwall. Further down the field, Jo Bonnier, in his first championship race, had taken over Luigi Villoresi's Maserati after four laps but had to retire himself just three laps later with valve trouble. And on lap six the Marquis de Portago's Lancia-Ferrari slid dramatically down the banking after losing a tyre and quit the race with a bent suspension.

Back at the sharp end, Castellotti lost another tyre on lap nine and retired after spinning wildly into the barrier, and two laps later Collins had to stop for a new tyre when lying in fourth. Then on lap 19, sensation. Fangio pulled into the pits with a broken steering arm. The damage could be repaired but the delay would wreck any chance Fangio had of winning the race. The pit signalled for Musso, who had moved up to third, to come in and hand over his car to Fangio so that the championship quest could be resumed, but Musso ignored the instruction and drove on.

Eventually, after four laps had been lost, Castellotti drove away in Fangio's repaired car, there being no point in Fangio returning to the fray so far adrift. As each lap passed the Argentinian could see his title hopes disappearing a little further. A world champion without a car.

Moss was now in the lead and pulling away from Schell. By half-distance the Englishman's advantage was 13 seconds. On lap 28 Schell stopped to refuel, promoting Musso to second, but two laps later Musso came in for a tyre check. Everyone expected that Fangio would take over, but Musso insisted on continuing. To Fangio's credit, he bore no malice.

Collins managed to get past Schell (who then retired on lap 32 with transmission trouble) and was still in third place on lap 35 when he came in for a tyre check. With Fangio seemingly out of the running, Collins had a very real chance of taking the title but when asked by Fangio's manager if he would consider handing his car over to the world champion, Collins did not hesitate. He jumped out of the cockpit, allowing Fangio to inherit third place. Fangio threw his arms around Collins in sheer exuberance and gratitude and sped off, hell-bent on making the most of his good fortune. Moss was still half a lap ahead of Musso until on lap 45 he ran out of fuel on the back straight. As the car slowed to around 120mph (193.1km/h), Moss spotted Luigi Piotti's privately entered Maserati coming up behind in seventh place and gestured to the Italian to give him a shove. The compliant Piotti tucked in behind Moss and proceeded to nudge the works Maserati round the curve to the pits, where Moss was able to refuel!

Moss rejoined in second place behind Musso but with only a ten-second margin over Fangio. Three laps from the finish, however, the steering arm on Musso's car broke as he was exiting the banking and he coasted to a halt in front of the pits. Despite a tyre that was almost bald, Moss held off Fangio's challenge to win by 5.7 seconds.

Moss took the race, Fangio the title, both having received a helping hand in different ways. Afterwards, track officials tried to disqualify Moss because he had been given a push, but Moss protested that Piotti was his team-mate and was therefore permitted to give him a push. In fact, Piotti was a privateer, but the officials swallowed the argument and allowed Moss's victory to stand. As for Collins, was his decision to throw away the chance of the championship an illustration of supreme sportsmanship or sheer stupidity? Collins tried to explain it away by saying that Fangio deserved the title and hinted that he (Collins) would never have been able to cope with the adulation anyway. Whether that would have been the case, we were never to know. For two years later, Collins was killed at the German Grand Prix before ever realising the chance to be world champion.

THE DAY
THE TRACK MELTED
FRENCH GRAND PRIX, 5 JULY 1959

Apart from two excursions to Rouen, the fast, triangular circuit at Reims was the home of the French Grand Prix throughout the 1950s. Never a place for the faint-hearted, Reims provided a greater challenge than usual in 1959 when temperatures soared so high that on race day the surface of the circuit started to melt.

The third race of the season following Monaco and Holland, Reims was expected to suit the Ferraris of Tony Brooks, Phil Hill and Jean Behra, and so it proved in the Wednesday practice session with Brooks setting a time of 2min 19.4sec which only Stirling Moss in a BRM could get near. Brooks and Moss were so content with their times that they sat out Thursday practice, during which Brabham's Cooper and Phil Hill nipped ahead of Moss to record the second and third fastest times respectively. These positions remained unaltered on the Friday and, with Saturday free, race day on the Sunday saw Brooks, Brabham and Hill line up on the front row with Moss and Behra on row two. Friday had been hot, but Sunday was even worse and by lunchtime the tarmac on parts of the circuit was beginning to melt in the extreme heat. How it would stand up to 50 laps remained to be seen.

The start was at 2p.m., and from the flag Brooks went straight into the lead with Moss surging through from the second rank. As the cars passed the grandstands for the first time Brooks still led from Moss, the American Masten Gregory (Cooper-Climax), Brabham and Phil Hill. Already the surface at Thillois hairpin was starting to break up and soon big stones and lumps of tar were being thrown up by the tyres. As the drivers suffered, Innes Ireland (Lotus) was the first to stop for replacement goggles. On lap eight Graham Hill brought his Lotus into the pits with a stone through the radiator and on the next lap Gregory stopped with a badly cut face and the effects of heat exhaustion.

By the tenth lap Brooks had a four-second lead over Maurice Trintignant's Cooper, followed by Brabham, Moss, Phil Hill and crowd favourite Behra, who had fought his way through the pack after stalling on the starting grid and having to be push-started. On lap 20 Trintignant spun at Thillois and stalled. Although he managed to push-start the car he was so tired that he had to stop at the pits for refreshment before resuming in twelfth place. By halfway Behra had worked his way up to fourth, but he had to retire on lap 32 when his engine blew.

All of the drivers were struggling in the intense heat. Brabham recalled: 'I was almost at the stage of collapsing at the wheel, so I broke all the windscreen away with my hand to try to get some air. Every car I got near showered me with bricks and stones. I was coasting into the corners rather than braking, because my feet were so badly burnt that I could hardly put any pressure on the pedals.'

Brabham's discomfort was heightened when Phil Hill passed him as, on lap 38, did Moss. However five laps later Moss stalled at Thillois and, unable to restart without outside assistance, was automatically disqualified. With the circuit continuing to disintegrate, Brooks picked his way around to win from Phil Hill and Brabham, the Australian having to be lifted out of the cockpit at the end of the race. The scene in the pits afterwards was likened to a hospital, with nearly every driver suffering from cuts and bruises caused by flying stones and tar, as well as the heat.

THE FINAL PUSH
UNITED STATES GRAND PRIX,
12 DECEMBER 1959

The final race of the 1959 Formula One season was the United States Grand Prix at Sebring, Florida – the first time that race had counted towards the World Drivers' Championship. Going into it, three drivers still had a chance of winning the title – Jack Brabham (in the revolutionary, rear-engined Cooper-Climax), Stirling Moss (Cooper-Climax) and Tony Brooks (Ferrari). With the best five finishes from the nine races counting, Brabham was six points ahead of Moss and eight ahead of Brooks, but the permutations were such that Moss could snatch the championship with a win and a fastest lap (provided Brabham didn't finish second) and Brooks could tie with the Australian if he won and Brabham failed to score.

During qualifying Brabham was unhappy with his car and decided to swap with his team-mate, 22-year-old New Zealander Bruce McLaren. But this car also needed some fine tuning and Brabham and the mechanics were up until one o'clock on the morning of the race. Grid position was all-important, but here the colourful American Harry Schell threw a spanner into the works by recording what appeared to be an unfeasibly fast time in his very moderate Cooper. Rumours circulated that he had taken a short cut along the back stretch of the bland airfield circuit, but Schell pleaded his innocence. His time of 3min 5.2sec (the third fastest, just ahead of Brooks) seemed too good to be true and

Ferrari, who naturally wanted Brooks on the three-car front row, immediately protested. After much argument, Schell insisted on taking his place on the front row alongside Moss and Brabham, thereby relegating Brooks to the second rank. Ferrari were not happy.

The race was to be run over 42 laps (218 miles/351km), and as the flag fell Brabham roared into the lead, only to be quickly passed by Moss. On the first lap Taffy von Trips accidentally rammed his Ferrari team-mate Brooks going into a corner and both went off. This was not the start Ferrari wanted and, after coming into the pits for a precautionary check, Brooks rejoined in a lowly fifteenth. Of course, if Brooks had been allowed to start on the front row he would, in all probability, have been well clear of von Trips, who started from row three. But for the time being, speculation could wait for another day.

By the fifth lap Moss had increased his lead to ten seconds but the next time round he coasted to a halt with a broken transmission. It would not be the first or the last time that Moss would stand accused of wrecking a car by setting off too quickly, but more important than the whys or the wherefores was the fact that he was now out of the championship equation. Brabham and McLaren proceeded to pull well clear with the race – and the title – seemingly sewn up. By the end of lap 24 there were only seven cars still running. Brooks did his utmost to make up the lost ground, but the deficit was too great and he was left languishing over a minute behind the leading pair in fifth. Although the race appeared to be in his pocket, Brabham was taking no chances and let McLaren slipstream him so that if anything should happen to the leading car, the New Zealander could take over at the front and still beat Brooks to the finish.

Starting the final lap, less than five seconds separated the front three of Brabham, McLaren and Maurice Trintignant, also in a Cooper. Then about 1 mile (1.6km) from the finish and with victory almost in sight, Brabham's car suddenly began to run on two cylinders. The engine went dead. He was out of fuel. McLaren slowed in sympathy, but Brabham frantically waved him on, fearing that Brooks might somehow snatch an unlikely win. McLaren got the message. Trintignant sped past moments afterwards as Brabham's car crawled around the track, eventually grinding to a complete halt some 500 yards (457m) from the finish. He took off his helmet and goggles, climbed out of the car and started to push. 'Why must home straights always be uphill?' he later lamented.

With McLaren and Trintignant already finished, the crowd wondered anxiously what had happened to Brabham. All eyes looked down the track. Then in the distance they spotted a hunched figure in blue overalls pushing his car up the straight. Brooks flashed by to take third and Brabham inched slowly but surely towards the line, encouraged in his efforts by the man waving the chequered flag. Police on motorcycles kept back the excited spectators, who were all too eager to give the weary Australian a helping hand which would probably have resulted in his disqualification. As Brabham himself remarked: 'It must have been the first time the new world champion was escorted to the line by a motorcycle escort.' After five minutes of pushing, he made it across the line and slumped to the ground in exhaustion … safe in the knowledge that he had won the World Championship by four points. It was a most unusual end to a season.

BRABHAM GOES BY TRAM
PORTUGUESE GRAND PRIX,
13 AUGUST 1960

After a faltering start to the defence of his title with
disappointments in Argentina and Monaco, Jack Brabham
struck a rich vein of form in mid-season, steering the
Cooper to victories in four successive Grands Prix –
Holland, Belgium, France and Britain. With three races left
and Brabham in a commanding position, the championship
moved to the street circuit of Oporto for the Portuguese
Grand Prix. Each 4⅔ mile (7.4km) lap presented a variety
of challenges for driver and car, not least cobblestones and
tramlines. It was likely to be a bumpy ride.

Among the 15 starters for the 55-lap race were Stirling
Moss, recovered from a crash at Spa when a wheel came off,
and world motorcycle champion John Surtees in only his
second four-wheel Grand Prix. To the surprise of many who
thought he would struggle to make the transformation to
cars, Surtees put his Lotus on pole, ahead of Dan Gurney's
BRM, Brabham and Moss. On the third row, Scotsman
Innes Ireland was puzzled to see an Irish flag fluttering
above his Lotus, the race organisers having deduced from
his surname that he was Irish!

Having stalled his engine on the grid in the previous race
(the British Grand Prix), Graham Hill was determined not
to miss out again and edged the BRM forward from the
second row while waiting for the flag to fall. Finding Hill
at their shoulder, the drivers ahead also inched forward so

that by the time the flag eventually fell, the entire front row plus Hill were a good car's length over the line. Gurney shot into the lead, only for Brabham to overhaul him at the first corner. Undaunted, Gurney fought back immediately and regained the lead under braking at the end of the straight. And so it was Gurney out in front at the start of a highly eventful lap two.

'After the straight and the left-hander,' remembered Brabham, 'you go uphill and along the tramlines. Then you have to turn left but the tramlines go straight on. I came up and moved inside to overtake but I got myself into the tramlines going straight on like a tram and it was obvious I wouldn't be able to stop. I thought, I'll have to stay in the tramlines all the way to the depot, wherever that is.' Finally he slowed and managed to extricate the Cooper before turning round and heading back towards the circuit. The crazy detour had cost him six places, plunging him from second to eighth.

After five laps Gurney led Surtees by five seconds with Moss in third, but on lap 11 Gurney spun and fell back to fifth. He later retired on lap 25 with engine trouble. Moss was hampered by similar problems which required a number of pit stops, so that at halfway Surtees held a comfortable lead from Phil Hill and Brabham. These two had been enjoying quite a scrap until, on lap 29, Hill missed a gear and ended up among the straw bales which had been spread liberally around the edge of the course as a safety feature.

Almost from the outset fuel had been seeping on to Surtees' canvas driving shoes and on lap 36 this caused his foot to slip off the brake pedal as he was approaching a twisty section. The car hit a kerb, the collision bursting the radiator. With Surtees out of the race, Brabham now led by a minute from his team-mate Bruce McLaren and, after his earlier adventures, the reigning champion was not going to let it slip. The Coopers came home in that order for Brabham's fifth Grand Prix win in a row and his second successive World Drivers' Championship. Fighting food poisoning to finish third at Oporto (which must have made every cobblestone a particularly unpleasant experience) was young Lotus driver Jim Clark in his first full season.

Meanwhile Moss ensured that the race concluded in almost as much chaos as it had started. He was lying in fifth on lap 51 when his brakes locked entering a corner. After stalling the car, he tried to restart, but while he was struggling the race finished. Realising this, he turned the car in the opposite direction, restarted it downhill, did a U-turn and crossed the line to finish what he thought was an ingenious fifth. Alas, his initiative was not rewarded and he was subsequently disqualified for driving in the wrong direction.

THE POST-RACE COLLISION

FRENCH GRAND PRIX, 8 JULY 1962

It is virtually unheard of for two Grand Prix cars to crash into each other *after* the race has finished, but that is precisely what happened at the end of an eventful 1962 French Grand Prix.

The race was returning to Rouen for the first time in five years, but without the Ferraris because of a strike in Italy. For this, the fourth race of the World Championship season, Jim Clark put the new Lotus 25 on pole, ahead of Graham Hill's BRM and Bruce McLaren's Cooper. The three drivers each had a win to their credit that year. Hill crossed the line first in the Dutch Grand Prix at Zandvoort, McLaren emerged victorious in Monaco and, three weeks before Rouen, Clark had picked up his first championship win, at Spa. And now just 0.6 seconds separated the three different marques on the front row in France.

Hill got away first from Clark and McLaren but his BRM team-mate Richie Ginther stalled on the grid and had to be pushed to the pits, finally joining the race almost a lap in arrears. By lap three of 54, John Surtees' Lola had moved up to second and was threatening Hill but a pit stop through fuel starvation on unlucky lap 13 dropped Surtees back to eighth. The Coopers were also proving surprisingly unreliable. Jack Brabham had to retire on lap 11 with a collapsed rear suspension and McLaren's car was plagued with the same problem. Although the New Zealander was able to rejoin the race, the delay had cost him any realistic chance of victory.

Up front, Hill had pulled out a healthy 22-second lead over Clark by lap 30. He had just lapped Jack Lewis for the second time when the Cooper's brakes failed and the car rammed Hill's BRM under braking for the next corner, sending Hill in a spin. This mishap enabled Clark to sneak through, only for the Scot to retire three laps later with a faulty front suspension. With 12 laps remaining and a 25-second advantage over Dan Gurney's Porsche, Hill seemed assured of his second win of the year, but then the BRM developed a fuel-injection difficulty and came to a halt at the hairpin, allowing Gurney to go on and gain his and Porsche's first championship victory. Having fought his way back up through the field, Surtees slipped down again with gearbox trouble, and so South African Tony Maggs was able to finish a surprise second in a Cooper, a lap behind the winner. Ginther was a further lap back in third.

But the real drama of the race was yet to come. As Surtees crossed the line in fifth and headed for the pits, he found his way blocked. At that point, Maurice Trintignant's Rob Walker-entered Lotus came rushing through in seventh and, swerving to avoid Surtees, left eighth-finisher Trevor Taylor in a works Lotus with nowhere to go. Taylor smashed into Trintignant at 80mph (128.7km/h), wrecking both cars but fortunately causing no lasting damage to either himself or the Frenchman. It was an expensive end to the day for both Rob Walker and Lotus.

THE GREAT ESCAPE
MONACO GRAND PRIX, 30 MAY 1965

Graham Hill and Monaco were made for each other. That raffish air, the fast life, the glitz, the glamour, no wonder it was his favourite circuit. Of his five wins there, he always rated his 1965 victory to be the finest – largely because he achieved it despite finding himself up an escape road a quarter of the way through the race.

Precision is the key to Monte Carlo. As Hill himself once remarked, there is nowhere to spin. If you get a corner slightly wrong, you run the risk of bouncing off hotels, nightclubs, telegraph poles or street lamps. Every yard of the 195 miles (314km) requires absolute concentration.

The 1965 World Championship was a stuttering affair. The first race had been on New Year's Day in South Africa where Jim Clark had won in a Lotus. The second race – at Monaco – was five months later, but Clark was absent on Indianapolis 500 duty. Having won there for the two previous years, Hill was hot favourite and sure enough he put the BRM on pole from Jack Brabham, now driving a car bearing his name. Both Brabham and Hill had new team-mates, of whom much more would be heard in years to come. With Dan Gurney also at Indianapolis, the second Brabham-Climax was driven for the first time in a championship race by New Zealander Denny Hulme. And Hill was partnered by a young Scotsman, Jackie Stewart, who excelled himself to go third fastest in the BRM in only his second Grand

Prix. Indeed on Friday practice Stewart had announced his arrival in no uncertain terms by actually going 0.2 seconds faster than Hill, but the BRM team leader regained the initiative in final qualifying on the Saturday afternoon. At the back of the grid – on their Grand Prix debuts – were two Hondas. Since the team had been guaranteed two starting places, the unlucky Jochen Rindt in a Cooper was excluded despite having lapped faster than Richie Ginther's Honda. Ironically, Ginther retired at the end of the first lap with a broken driveshaft. Rindt's time would come.

Hill led from the start, pursued by Stewart, Lorenzo Bandini and John Surtees in the two Ferraris, and Brabham. The BRMs began to pull away from the Ferraris at the rate of about a second per lap and appeared to have everything in control. Then on lap 25, Hill came out of the tunnel at around 120mph (193.1km/h) and as he started to brake in readiness for the chicane, he saw Robert Anderson's Brabham approaching the chicane at a crawl, a universal joint having broken. Realising to his horror that Anderson was going to be occupying the chicane at precisely the same time that he intended to fly through it at 95mph (152.9km/h) and that there was only room for one car, Hill slammed on the brakes as hard as he could. He later wrote: 'I made as if to go through the chicane and I left things until the point of no return, and then I saw that there was just no way I could get through without clobbering him. I came off the brakes for a second so that I could steer and changed direction down the escape road. Then I stood on them again and I left some rare old skid marks.'

The BRM ground to a halt well up the escape road. Hill quickly jumped out of the car, pushed it backwards on to the track, climbed in again and restarted the engine, all of which took some 35 seconds and dropped him back to fifth behind Stewart, Bandini, Surtees and Brabham.

Cursing his luck, Hill set off in hot pursuit of the leaders. 'I was a bit cheesed off over the whole business,' he remarked. 'If I had come by a second later I would have been able to get through, but as it was, I just couldn't get down to a sufficiently slow pace to follow Anderson through the chicane at his speed. It was bad luck that he just happened to be in that position.'

On lap 30 Hill caught Stewart, who had spun away his lead at Sainte Devote, and four laps later the youngster moved over and waved his team leader through. Meanwhile Brabham passed both Ferrari to take the lead, only to drop out with engine trouble on lap 43. Hill was now third behind the two Ferraris and began attacking them for all he was worth, repeatedly shattering the lap record. He got past Surtees on lap 53 on the short downhill stretch leading from Casino Square, and after sitting patiently on Bandini's tail for 12 laps, he pounced on the Italian at the same spot. Surtees, too, overtook Bandini and actually closed to within two seconds of Hill but Hill reacted by setting another new lap record to reaffirm his position. Surtees' plucky drive came to an untimely end on the penultimate lap when he spluttered to a halt having run out of fuel, but as only Hill, Bandini and Stewart completed the full race distance, he was still classified fourth.

So Hill recorded an improbable victory, born out of adversity, and one which emphasised why he was the uncrowned King of Monaco. Overshadowing even his own little excursion, the most spectacular moment of the race occurred at the entrance to the chicane on lap 80 when Paul Hawkins' Lotus spun through the straw bales, went over the edge of the quay and ended up in the harbour in much the same manner as Alberto Ascari ten years earlier. Hawkins was unhurt, but as Hill could have testified, there were more practical ways of getting through the chicane in moments of crisis.

THE DEMOLITION INDY

INDIANAPOLIS 500, 30 MAY 1966

The Americans were hell-bent on revenge. They were still smarting from the previous year when Jim Clark had the effrontery to become the first British driver to win the Indianapolis 500. The US press had poured scorn on the Scotsman's chances before that race and had afterwards been forced to eat humble pie, never the most popular American dish. They were adamant that there would be no repeat performance in 1966. The Brits were going to be put in their place.

In the build-up to the world's largest single-day sporting event (attracting a crowd in excess of 400,000), the Americans were full of confidence despite a three-pronged British assault from Clark's Lotus, and the Lolas of Graham Hill and the emerging Jackie Stewart. Both Hill and Stewart were making their debuts at the Brickyard – in Stewart's case it would be his one and only appearance – but their drives would leave a lasting impression after a hugely eventful race in which most of the drama was packed into the start and finish.

The American talent on show included five cars from Dan Gurney's new Eagle team, but it was young Mario Andretti who took pole in a Brawner-Ford. Alongside him on the front row was Clark's Lotus, Hill qualifying a disappointing fifteenth. Right at the back of the grid was Bobby Grim's Watson-Offy, the only front-engined car in the race. The start could scarcely have been more sensational. Indianapolis was no stranger to spectacular pile-ups but this was extraordinary even by its standards. After just 100 yards (91.4m) Billy Foster and Gordon Johncock collided going into Turn One and 14 more cars piled into the wreckage, wheels flying in every direction. Some spectators were slightly hurt by flying debris but when the dust settled, the only permanent damage was to the 11 cars – a third of the field – which were eliminated. An hour and a half later the race was restarted. Andretti shot into the lead from Clark, while further back Hill had a tricky moment on Turn One when his car hit a patch of oil left over from the multiple crash. Andretti maintained his advantage until he was black-flagged with smoke pouring from his car, caused by a defective valve. Clark took over at the front but his hopes of a repeat victory were dashed by a spin on Turn Four on lap 62 which cost him 25 seconds and allowed Lloyd Ruby's Eagle to step into top spot. When Clark spun again on lap 84 and lost the best part of a minute in the pits, Stewart, who was enjoying a remarkable drive, went second. All three Brits were now very much in contention, Hill having moved steadily through the field, but at 350 miles (563km), Ruby looked the likely winner, only to be black-flagged himself due to the appearance of ominous clouds of smoke. Suddenly Stewart found himself in the lead, and there he stayed until just ten laps from the finish when he dropped out with engine failure. It was a cruel blow and he walked back to the pits to a tremendous ovation from the crowd who, in spite of their partisanship, were appreciative of what had been a courageous debut on arguably the world's most intimidating race track.

With Hill and Clark now vying for the lead, it seemed certain that victory would go to a British driver ... but which one? At the end of the race, by which time only seven cars were still running, both men thought they had won. Lotus team boss Colin Chapman told Clark that he was the winner and the Scot duly completed a lap of honour. However, Hill was equally sure that he had won and both cars headed for Victory Lane. The dispute concerned lap 175, on which Hill had passed Clark. Lotus insisted that Hill had merely unlapped himself but Lola thought Hill had been moving into second. Clark's sponsor, the forthright Andy Granatelli, stormed: 'How could Hill win when they were announcing and showing on the scoreboard that Stewart and Clark were running one-two and Hill was half a lap away on the backstretch? If that was the case, Hill had been leading all the time and Stewart was never in front. We lapped Hill on the forty-seventh lap and we were running faster than him the rest of the way.' When it was put to Hill that there had been a mix-up in the timekeepers' box, he simply brushed it aside.

The official timekeepers agreed with Hill and awarded him the race by 41.13 seconds from Clark. Granatelli backed down graciously, admitting that he had been as confused as everyone else. 'On the forty-seventh lap we lapped Graham Hill,' he said. 'On the fiftieth it was announced that we had lapped all but the first five and that Hill was running ninth. But when Clark spun on the sixty-second lap, Hill got by. We didn't see him do it and assumed Clark was still in front.'

In becoming the first rookie to win the 500 since George Souders in 1927, Hill averaged 144⅓mph (232.3km/h). So at the end of a race in which the first-corner carnage thereafter earned it the nickname of the 'Demolition Indy', the Americans were left licking their wounds for the second successive year. Hill mischievously suggested that in future they should award a trophy for the first American to finish. The reply was probably not printable.

A HARE'S BREADTH

ITALIAN GRAND PRIX,
7 SEPTEMBER 1969

Jackie Stewart's Matra had dominated the 1969 season. With victories in South Africa, Spain, Holland, France and Britain to his name, he had turned the Formula One World Drivers' Championship into a one-horse race. The only question to be answered was precisely when he would clinch the title. Following a rare display of fallibility when he retired at the German Grand Prix, Stewart and the circus moved to Monza. Even if he failed in Italy, there were still three more races to come but he had no intention of letting matters drag on unnecessarily. The Italian Grand Prix had a recent history of close finishes. Two years earlier John Surtees had pipped Jack Brabham by 0.2 seconds. This one would prove even tighter, with no fewer than four drivers harbouring hopes of victory going into the last corner of the last of the 68 laps.

Qualifying put Austrian Jochen Rindt on pole in a Lotus alongside the 1967 world champion Denny Hulme in a McLaren, while Stewart shared the second row with the Brabham of Briton Piers Courage. Rindt was first away, followed by Stewart, but the positions were reversed after the Lesmo Curves. With a clear road ahead of him on the second lap, Stewart spotted a tiny movement in the distance. It was a hare. Suddenly the animal darted towards the Matra. There was no chance – or indeed desire on a crowded race track – to take avoiding action and the hare smacked into one of the car's front tyres. Stewart's immediate concern was that a bone from the hare might cause a puncture. From then on, he closely monitored the shape of the tyre, looking for any sign of abnormality.

Before the inevitable chicane came to town, the high-speed Monza circuit was ideally tailored for slipstreaming and as the race unfolded, a gaggle of eight cars jostled for the lead – Stewart, Rindt, Hulme, Jean-Pierre Beltoise (Matra), Jo Siffert (Lotus), Bruce McLaren, Courage and Graham Hill (Lotus). Positions among this leading group chopped and changed on a regular basis but, one by one, Hulme, Siffert and Hill all fell away with mechanical trouble. Courage also slipped back, leaving the remaining quartet to fight it out. At the start of the last lap, the order was Stewart, Rindt, Beltoise, McLaren, with under half a second covering the four. Rindt snatched the lead at the sweeping right-hander, the Curva Grande, and held on through the Lesmo Curves but going into the long, final bend, the Curva Parabolica, both Stewart and Beltoise made their moves. Utilising Stewart's slipstream, Beltoise edged out and then dived inside, seizing the lead momentarily. But he had shown his hand too soon. The Frenchman's impetus carried him wider than he would have wished and Stewart was able to sneak up the inside with Rindt in his slipstream. Having prepared his car with a fourth-gear ratio specifically for such an eventuality, Stewart saw his decision bear fruit as he just managed to hold off Rindt on the 250 yard (229m) dash to the flag. They flashed across the line virtually side by side but Stewart had his nose in front by approximately half a length of racing car. The official distance was 0.08 seconds, at the time the closest-ever winning margin in a championship race. Beltoise was 0.09 seconds further back in third with McLaren a mere 0.02 seconds behind him. Thus the first four were covered by 0.19 seconds. It was that close.

So Stewart claimed his crown and the Italian crowd saw a tremendously exciting race. In fact the only real loser on the day was the hare.

ON TOW AROUND MONZA
CARAVAN SPEED TRIAL, MONZA, OCTOBER 1969

When Caravans International announced that it was staging a speed trial in which two cars would tow caravans around Monza for 5,000 miles (8,0476km) over a period of three and a half days, the first question on everyone's lips was: why? Perhaps the idea was in response to Jackie Stewart's concerns about Formula One safety – after all, giving a Ferrari or a Lotus a caravan to tow would certainly have had the desired effect of reducing speeds on Grand Prix circuits ... all the more so if the likes of Clay Regazzoni and Jacky Ickx had to stop every couple of laps to shut the caravan door! Instead it seems that the exercise was simply an attempt to demonstrate the reliability and durability of the humble caravan.

The two vehicles taking part were a Ford Cortina 1600 (towing a four-berth, 10-foot caravan) and a more powerful Ford Corsair 2000E (towing a bigger and therefore heavier four-berth caravan, 12ft 6in long). A team of nine drivers (including two reserves) was assembled to work in three-hour shifts. To qualify beforehand, the drivers had to do two laps without stopping at 37½mph (60.3km/h), then two laps at 44½mph (71.6km/h), and finally two laps at 52mph (83.7km/h). Obviously there was a little leeway either side of these figures.

One might think – and with some justification – that towing a caravan round and round a deserted race track for over three days and nights at a steady speed of 60mph (96.6km/h) would achieve a level of mind-blowing tedium normally reserved for Channel 5 entertainment shows. As a spectator sport, it would be considered on a par with tile-grouting or pro-celebrity ironing. Yet the event was far from incident-free, enlivened considerably by the hundreds of rabbits which come out to play when Monza is not invaded by the *tifosi*. Other things went bump in the night, notably a wolf-like animal which Alan Hayes hit at 2a.m. on the back straight while doing 70mph (112.7km/h). The Cortina suffered a little damage but was able to continue after a two-minute stop to straighten out the wing. The mystery beast was left at the side of the track. On another occasion Ian Mantle encountered two young motorcyclists trying to ride up and down the banking and was fortunate to be able to squeeze car and caravan through between them. And John Yoxall narrowly avoided a young woman who had tried climbing the banking on foot but was sliding down out of control …

An additional hazard was the fog which had a habit of descending on the circuit at night, making it not only difficult to spot the rabbits but also to maintain the speeds necessary to produce a healthy average rate. After two days the Corsair began to lose a little power and resorted to following in the Cortina's slipstream for long periods, but overall it was the bigger-engined car which came out on top. The Corsair (which made a total of 23 pit stops and lost 18 minutes for a generator change) covered the 5,000 miles in 81hr 22min at a speed of 61½mph (98.9km/h); the Cortina (with 27 pit stops) did the same distance in 82hr 47min at a speed of 60½mph (97.2km/h).

As for the caravans, they were towed impeccably throughout, any damage sustained being negligible. Happily, however, nobody present at Monza over those three days thought they had seen the future of motor racing.

PUNCH-UP AT THE PALACE

SHELL FORMULA THREE CHAMPIONSHIP, ROUND 11, 3 OCTOBER 1970

By 1970 James Hunt had only been racing for three years, but in that time he had already earned a reputation as someone whom trouble seemed to follow around. His proposed debut, at Snetterton in 1967, came to nought after he was refused permission to race because his Mini had no windows. Two years later he had worked his way up to Formula Ford but was prevented from taking part in a European Championship race at Vallelunga in Italy because he did not have the necessary medical certificate. His reaction was to sabotage the start of the race by deliberately parking his car at right angles across the front of the grid! As controversy continued to dog his every move, a fellow competitor's mother remarked that Hunt always carried £5 on him in those days so that he had enough money for a protest. He was never one to shrink away from confrontation.

By 1970 he had entered the ranks of Formula Three and was making people sit up and take notice for the right reasons. Competing in the Shell Formula Three Championship, he had scored points in five of the ten rounds, including a second at Oulton Park and a third at Cadwell Park. In between he had also posted his second major Formula Three win, in a non-championship race at Zolder in Belgium. So his star was definitely in the ascendant when he came to the compact Crystal Palace circuit in South London for round 11, the penultimate race in the series.

Driving a Lotus 59, Hunt finished second in his heat, thereby qualifying for the final. With BBC *Grandstand* cameras covering the event, there was huge anticipation that the drivers would put on a memorable show for the armchair audience. Hunt made sure the TV viewers got more than they bargained for.

Australian David Walker, lying second in the championship, took the race by the scruff of the neck and so the main interest centred on the six-car battle for second place, which included Hunt's Lotus and a March 703 driven by Dave Morgan. Approaching the last corner on the penultimate lap, the two cars were virtually abreast but Hunt appeared to have the better line. However Morgan refused to yield, with the result that the pair collided, the Lotus ending up in the middle of the track and the March embedded in the pit wall, both minus one wheel. Hunt exploded, leapt from his car, rushed over to Morgan and lunged at him, aiming a punch which, perhaps fortunately for both parties, missed by a country mile. Morgan recalled: 'The silly arse leapt out of his car and ran across the track, all these racing cars coming past him. I was amazed he wasn't run over. I was trying to undo my helmet and as he turned to punch me I lost my balance and fell so he missed. Then other people got hold of him and dragged him off.'

Autosport wrote that 'a justifiably enraged Hunt felled Morgan in the heat of the moment' but *Motor Sport* adopted a less partisan line, reporting: 'A stewards' enquiry was convened but by then Hunt had regrettably resorted to fisticuffs to settle his differences. This is very much against the spirit of camaraderie which exists in motor racing and was greatly deplored.'

Hunt was widely pilloried over his latest transgression by people who saw him as a hot-headed upstart who was bringing the sport into disrepute. Hunt protested his innocence and at the subsequent RAC tribunal, which both drivers were summoned to attend, he produced BBC footage of the incident. This clearly showed that his car had not hit Morgan's first. Furthermore three other drivers testified that, in their opinion, Morgan had overtaken in a dangerous manner. Consequently the outcome of the tribunal was that Hunt was exonerated and Morgan was banned for a year.

For Hunt at least, the punch-up at the Palace had a happy ending. But it would by no means be his last brush with authority.

MAD DOGS AND MEXICANS
MEXICAN GRAND PRIX,
25 OCTOBER 1970

The 1970 Formula One season was a sad one, the death of Jochen Rindt at the Italian Grand Prix resulting in the first posthumous world champion. The year ended in turmoil with a chaotic Mexican Grand Prix which posed serious questions about the control of both humans and animals.

There were only 18 starters for the 65 laps of the Mexico City track as the organisers, on a limited budget, still adhered to the practice of paying starting money rather than allocating prize money according to finishing order. At 44, Jack Brabham had announced that this would be his final race but he showed no sign of easing up and made fourth fastest on the grid behind Clay Regazzoni (Ferrari), Jackie Stewart (Tyrrell), and Jacky Ickx in the second Ferrari. As expected, race day was warm and sunny, but what nobody had anticipated was that a crowd of around 200,000 would turn up to watch an essentially meaningless race. As the start time drew nearer, the spectators became increasingly unruly and began tearing down safety fences and barriers to obtain a trackside view. Soon rows and rows of them were standing, tightly packed, on the very edge of the circuit. When it was announced that the start would be delayed so that the crowd could be moved back, bottles were thrown on to the track in protest.

The race might well have been called off but for the very real fear that a cancellation would have provoked a full-scale riot, so instead Stewart and Mexican driver Pedro Rodriguez toured the circuit, appealing to the crowd to move back a little behind the barriers. Even this extremely reasonable request had little effect, but, after the broken bottles had been swept up, the drivers came out for an inspection lap. Although some still harboured reservations, the situation was thought to be just about under control and the race was quickly started – well over an hour late.

Regazzoni led into the first turn but by the end of the second lap he had been overtaken by both Ickx and Stewart. On lap 14 Stewart's steering column worked loose, and the resultant pit stop cost him almost exactly one lap and relegated him to last but one place. Stewart rejoined the race right behind third-placed Brabham on the road and wasted no time in unlapping himself from both Brabham and Regazzoni. At half-distance Ickx was 15 seconds ahead of Regazzoni, who in turn led Brabham by another 12 seconds. Having worked his way up to tenth, Stewart then fell foul of a marauding Mexican dog which ran on to the track in front of the Tyrrell and bent the car's front suspension. A forlorn Stewart had no option but to retire.

Brabham kept plugging away in typical fashion until on lap 53 his engine blew up to deny him the farewell for which he had been hoping. The two Ferraris were now out on their own and Ickx came home the best part of a minute ahead of Regazzoni, with Denny Hulme's McLaren back in third.

Over the closing laps the crowd had once again pushed forward to the edge of the track, and no sooner had Ickx taken the chequered flag than they swarmed all over the circuit, forcing the remaining cars to slow right down in order to avoid any number of accidents.

The repercussions of the crowd behaviour were severe. The International Sporting Commission cancelled the 1971 Mexican Grand Prix when it was unable to obtain a guarantee from the organisers that there would be no repeat of the 1970 farce, and it turned out to be another 15 years before the event was finally restored to the motor-racing calendar.

THE RALLY WITH NO FINISHERS

BANDAMA RALLY, DECEMBER 1972

The organiser of the daunting Liège-Rome-Liège Rally once proclaimed that his ideal was to create an event with single-figure finishers. Well, the brains behind the 1972 Bandama Rally in West Africa went one better by producing such a punishing schedule that there were no finishers at all!

This was only the second-ever Bandama Rally. When Bob Neyret won the 1971 event in a Peugeot 504, the result hardly warranted a mention, but the following year the rally achieved instant notoriety.

A total of 52 cars set out, but a schedule which most of the drivers described as 'ludicrous' quickly saw wholesale eliminations. When the teams protested that the time limits were virtually impossible to meet, the organisers simply shrugged their shoulders and flatly refused to modify the targets. Shekhar Mehta in a Datsun 240Z did manage to complete the route but was adjudged to be out of time, while Tony Fall in a Peugeot 504 actually finished within the time limits, only for the entire results to be scrapped following protests from the aggrieved Renault team.

In what was probably an attempt to distance itself from the 1972 fiasco, the event was subsequently renamed the Ivory Coast Rally.

THROUGH THE BARRICADES

MONTE CARLO RALLY, JANUARY 1973

A total of 278 starters set off from such diverse cities as Athens, Glasgow, Frankfurt, Oslo, Rome and Warsaw to take part in the 1973 Monte Carlo Rally. Yet only 51 made it through to the Mediterranean as mass disqualification led to barricades being manned by protesting drivers and patrolled by armed police in what became an additional – and unforeseen – hazard in the world's showpiece rally.

That year's Common Route – to be taken by all competitors – began at the French town of Alès and consisted of ten stages over a distance of 1,040 miles (1,674km). The day before the Common Route was due to begin, however, three of the stages were blocked by snow, among them the third stage, the Burzet loop. This section had been blocked for several days prior to the rally and although no fresh snow had fallen in the meantime, the strong wind had prevented the road from being cleared. Competitors waiting for the Common Route to begin heard about the problem via advance ice-note crews who had been unable to get through, and so it was generally assumed that the rally would be rerouted. And when there was no news of a reroute, they deduced – not unreasonably – that conditions on the Burzet stage must have improved. In fact a snow plough had been sent out to try and create a way through, but as soon as it cleared a path, the wind blew the snow back on to the road. Feelings were already running high over a proposal that studs should be banned on the special stage across the Col du Corobin between Digne and Monte Carlo. Factory teams and tyre companies launched an immediate objection, and the proposal was scrapped. But it was an indication that all was not sweetness and light in the world of rallying that year.

In spite of the snow, the Burzet stage went ahead. Sixty-five cars managed to pick a way through before a Capri spun and wedged itself between two snow banks, rendering the road completely impassable. For some inexplicable reason, however, the marshals at the start of the stage kept sending competitors in, with the result that there was soon a nose-to-tail jam of rally cars with nowhere to go. To compound their blunder, the rally organisers ruled that no extra time allowance would be given. Consequently the 144 cars stuck behind the Capri were all disqualified, not only because they had failed to complete the stage but also because they were over the set time limits.

The excluded crews, many of whom had spent a fortune travelling across Europe in order to compete, were outraged at the organisers' intransigence and decided that if they were not going to be allowed to finish the rally, nobody else would be either. So they raced off to Digne and set up barricades across the road leading into the town, the idea being to delay the remaining competitors until they, too, were over the time limit. Learning of the proposed sabotage, the organisers alerted the French police who despatched vanloads of gendarmes with orders to stop all but the surviving crews from reaching the Digne road. But by the time the police arrived on the scene, the barricades were already in place. The protesters dug in for a pitched battle, if necessary, leaving those who intended completing the rally to find ingenious methods of circumnavigating the blockade. Timo Makinen got through by driving his Escort directly at the barricade before veering up a steep bank at the last minute and flying past the frustrated pickets.

Rauno Aaltonen opted for a more extreme detour. Revving the engine of his Datsun, he mounted a bank, burst through a hedge, drove across a field, jumped a ditch, and emerged through the hedge on the other side, having neatly sidestepped the protesters.

Sometimes the mood turned ugly. Two women competitors, furious at the bar to their progress, were further enraged when a pair of pistol-waving gendarmes insisted that the barricade be lifted to allow a local shopper through in her 2CV. The driver of the rally car promptly stood in front of the 2CV and refused to let it move until she was allowed to follow. The police threatened retribution, but were eventually forced to back down and let both cars through.

As the remnants of the rally soldiered on towards Monte Carlo, Makinen's hopes were hit when he lost a front wheel ... and five minutes while a spare was being fitted. The snowy conditions favoured the Alpine-Renaults, who were able to make considerable ground on the Common Route and ended up filling five of the first six places in the final classification. Makinen's delay handed victory to the Alpine of Jean-Claude Andruet and co-driver Michele Petit (who used the pseudonym 'Biche'). They finished 26 seconds ahead of Ove Andersson's Alpine.

The end of the rally did not bring about an end to hostilities and the winter of discontent rumbled on. As a peace gesture, the organisers offered the disqualified crews free entries for the 1974 Monte. But the energy crisis meant that the rally never took place. Some disputes are simply not meant to be resolved amicably.

SAFETY FIRST

CANADIAN GRAND PRIX,
23 SEPTEMBER 1973

The penultimate race in the 1973 Formula One World Championship season at the Mosport Park circuit near Toronto marked the first occasion on which a safety car was used in a Grand Prix. It was not exactly an auspicious beginning, the car's introduction creating wholesale confusion which lasted until long after the chequered flag had been shown.

With Jackie Stewart having already clinched his third drivers' title, the outcome of the Canadian Grand Prix was academic apart from whether Tyrrell or Lotus would take the constructors' title. In misty, damp conditions Ronnie Peterson put his JPS Lotus on pole, ahead of the McLarens of Peter Revson and Jody Scheckter. Race morning produced heavy rain, turning the untimed practice session into a lottery as a succession of cars spun off. The conditions were so appalling that the organisers allowed three exploratory laps before the race finally got under way 40 minutes late.

Peterson was first away in a plume of spray but the Swede was on Goodyear tyres, and judging by the way that Niki Lauda on Firestones had come through from the fourth row on the grid to be third at the end of the opening lap, it was quickly clear that these were better suited to the wet track. On lap three Lauda's BRM calmly went past Scheckter and Peterson to take the lead and proceeded to draw away at the extraordinary rate of four seconds per lap. With cars spinning at regular intervals, Peterson lurched into a guard rail on lap 17 because of a deflating tyre, but as the track began to dry out, Lauda dived into the pits three laps later to change to intermediate tyres. When the Austrian rejoined the race, he had dropped to eighth behind Emerson Fittipaldi (JPS Lotus), Jackie Oliver (Shadow), François Cevert (Tyrrell), Scheckter, Stewart (Tyrrell), Howden Ganley (Williams) and Carlos Reutemann (Brabham).

The pits were now full of drivers changing from wets to intermediates, with the result that it became difficult to know who was actually leading the race. When the leaders came in, Jean-Pierre Beltoise's BRM took over briefly until he, too, pitted. In this state of confusion when some of the front-runners had come in and others hadn't, Scheckter and Cevert collided going into Turn Two on lap 33 while battling for fourth place. Although neither driver was badly injured, their damaged cars partially blocked the track, bringing the safety car into play for the first time. The driver of the safety vehicle waved a number of cars past until, to the surprise of just about everyone, it took up station immediately ahead of Ganley. The New Zealander had started three rows from the back of the grid and was not leading by anyone's calculations … except, apparently, those of the safety driver. Stewart and Fittipaldi were tucked in behind Ganley and an orderly queue duly formed. Those who capitalised most from the situation were Revson and Oliver who, being just ahead of Ganley, were able to continue at normal race speed until they fell in at the back of the 21-car queue. Meanwhile argument was raging in the pits as to who was leading. Was it Fittipaldi? Or Oliver? Or Revson? The only thing the teams seemed to agree upon was that it definitely wasn't Howden Ganley.

When the safety car eventually turned off, Ganley proceeded to drive an inspired race, holding Stewart and Fittipaldi at bay for eight laps. By now the general consensus of opinion was that the real race leader was Oliver, with

Fittipaldi second nearly a lap behind, but nobody could be sure. Fittipaldi soon passed Stewart and began to rein in Oliver, who lost precious seconds on lap 47 when the Shadow developed sticking throttle slides. By lap 76 – with just four to go – excitement was high as Fittipaldi and Oliver ran nose to tail. But what neither they nor any of the spectators knew was that they weren't battling for the lead at all – they were competing for second place.

On the penultimate lap Fittipaldi managed to pass Oliver and held on to what he thought was the finish. As the Brazilian crossed the line, Lotus team chief Colin Chapman threw his cap into the air in celebration ... but there was no sign of the chequered flag. Half a lap later the flag was suddenly waved at a gaggle of cars comprising Ganley, Revson, James Hunt, Reutemann and Mike Hailwood. With Lotus still claiming a Fittipaldi win, it emerged that the flag was meant for Revson who had gained virtually a whole lap when the safety car picked up the wrong car! Fittipaldi had, in fact, been a lap behind when the safety car left the track.

Amid much discussion, interspersed with occasional acrimony, the winner's trophy was presented to Revson. Three hours later, when all the drivers' lap times had been examined and re-examined, the American was confirmed as the winner with Fittipaldi second and Oliver third. Having tasted his 15 minutes of fame, Ganley was officially placed sixth.

At the inquest into the confusion, it was generally accepted that the safety car principle was fine ... but that it would help if in future it picked up the right car.

STUCK IN THE PIT LANE

BRITISH GRAND PRIX, 20 JULY 1974

The British Grand Prix at Brands Hatch was the tenth race of the 1974 Formula One World Championship. After a dismal 1973, Ferrari was on the way up again, thanks largely to the efforts of Niki Lauda whose victories in Spain and Holland had put him at the head of the contest for the drivers' title. In qualifying at the Kent circuit, Lauda met a formidable opponent in Sweden's Ronnie Peterson and the Ferrari and the Lotus ended up tying for pole position. The second row consisted of Jody Scheckter's Tyrrell and Carlos Reutemann's Brabham, while home eyes were focused on row three where James Hunt's Hesketh lined up alongside the Shadow of young Welshman Tom Pryce, who had already won the 100 bottles of champagne presented by the *Evening News* for the fastest lap during the Thursday morning practice session. Even as the cars left the pits before the start there was drama, Hunt's Hesketh hitting a Tyrrell mechanic and breaking both his legs. The crowded pit lane would be a foretaste of things to come.

At the end of the first of the 75 laps, Lauda held a two-second lead over Scheckter, ahead of Clay Regazzoni, who had shot up from the fourth row, and Peterson. Lauda and Scheckter pulled away steadily from the chasing pack, many of whom were being crippled by punctures. As early as lap 19 John Watson in a privately entered Brabham called into the pits with a puncture, caused by the proliferation of small flinty stones on the track, and over the next few laps five more drivers, including Regazzoni, Peterson and Graham Hill, were all forced to stop with deflated tyres. Out in front Lauda remained unruffled, his lead having stretched to a comfortable eight seconds, but then on lap 55 he, too, sustained a slow puncture. The previously smooth-running Ferrari began to handle erratically. His pit signalled that they had a new tyre ready and urged him to come in, but Lauda was desperate for championship points and knew that a stop at that stage would as good as hand the race to Scheckter. So he made a calculated decision to try and hold out to the finish.

It was not to be. Scheckter closed relentlessly and, five laps from the end, capitalised on Lauda's misfortune to sweep past into the lead. Lauda soldiered on gamely but two laps later Emerson Fittipaldi relegated him to third. Then on the penultimate lap the tyre finally burst. Bits of rubber were flying everywhere, leaving Lauda no option but to rumble into the pits on the flat. The Ferrari crew changed the tyre in 20 seconds but as Lauda accelerated away to rejoin the race, he found his way barred by crowds of people who had flooded the pit lane to watch Scheckter take the chequered flag. To make matters worse, an RAC official had backed his Ford Cortina across the exit in readiness for the winner's lap of honour. Fearing an accident, a marshal rushed out and showed Lauda the red flag, whereupon the Austrian climbed out of his car and stormed off.

The red flag signalling the immediate end of the race gave Lauda a finishing position of ninth (and therefore no championship points). Ferrari protested but the RAC stewards dismissed it, so Ferrari appealed to the sport's governing body, the FIA. They elevated Lauda to fifth (and two points) on the grounds that the red flag had been shown incorrectly. It was a chaotic end to a Grand Prix, and ultimately the two points which Lauda clawed back made no difference to the outcome of the championship as Fittipaldi took the title with something to spare.

HALF POINTS IN BARCELONA

SPANISH GRAND PRIX, 27 APRIL 1975

Set within picturesque parkland near Barcelona, the 2⅓ mile (3.8km) Montjuich Park circuit first hosted the Spanish Grand Prix in 1969. On that occasion both Graham Hill and Jochen Rindt were involved in high-speed crashes when their Lotuses experienced identical wing failure over the same crest. For the next six years, it alternated with Jarama as the venue for Spain's premier motor race, but the events of 1975 brought its brief career as a Grand Prix circuit to an abrupt end.

Safety concerns were voiced during practice and on the eve of qualifying the Grand Prix Drivers' Association safety committee inspected the track. It found that bolts were missing from much of the Armco barrier, as a result of which the drivers announced that they would refuse to race until the bolts were inserted. When the organisers immediately threatened to seize the cars and equipment to cover their contractual losses, the team owners brought pressure on their drivers to take part. The drivers backed down ... reluctantly. Reigning world champion Emerson Fittipaldi would complete just three slow laps – sufficient to guarantee McLaren its starting money – before sitting out the rest of the race in protest.

An accident occurred within seconds of the start. Braking into the first corner, Niki Lauda's Ferrari was rammed from behind by Mario Andretti's Parnelli as the American tried to force his way to the front. The Ferrari spun sideways and out of the race. In trying to take avoiding action, Lauda's team-mate, Clay Regazzoni, sustained a damaged front wheel and nose cone and had to limp to the pits for repairs. He eventually rejoined the action four laps adrift. Hesketh driver James Hunt was the principal beneficiary of the first-corner smash, scrambling through a gap to lead at the end of the opening lap from Andretti, and John Watson in a Surtees.

Spilt oil on the track was now providing an extra hazard. On lap seven Hunt hit the oil slick, slammed into the barrier and retired. Watson proceeded to hit the barrier at almost the same point, but not quite as forcefully, and managed to hold on to second behind Andretti for four more laps until the car's handling deteriorated to such an extent that he was forced to call into the pits. By lap 17 Andretti had a 20-second lead over Rolf Stommelen's Hill-Ford, the Brabham of Carlos Pace and Ronnie Peterson in a JPS Lotus. But then it was Andretti's turn to smash into a guard rail and out of the race. On lap 24 Peterson retired, promoting Jochen Mass (McLaren) to third and Jacky Ickx (Lotus) to fourth.

Two laps later came the big accident that everyone had been dreading. Shortly after making a pit stop, Stommelen was travelling at 150mph (241.4km/h) when the wing of his Hill-Ford came loose. The car veered out of control and smashed into the safety barrier, killing four people who were standing behind it – a track marshal, two fire marshals and a photographer. Pace, close behind in second, braked hard and swerved but was struck by the half-airborne car as it came back across the road. The Brabham was sent sliding into the Armco but Pace was unhurt. Stommelen, however, sustained a broken leg. By a macabre coincidence, the car owned by Graham Hill had suffered the same accident as the one he was driving in 1969 ... and over the same crest.

The yellow flags were brought out but in the confusion

a number of drivers ignored them. Three laps later the organisers waved the cars down and stopped the race. At the time Mass was leading and so he was declared the winner from Ickx, Carlos Reutemann (Brabham), Jean-Pierre Jarier (Shadow) and Vittorio Brambilla (March). But as just 29 of the scheduled 75 laps had been completed, the drivers were only awarded half the normal points.

There was one happy story to emerge from the shambles of Montjuich Park. Sixth place was filled by Lella Lombardi in a March, who thus became the first, and so far only, woman to score a Formula One World Championship point … or, more precisely, a World Championship half-point.

VICTORY IN SLOW MOTION
DAYTONA 500, 15 FEBRUARY 1976

The jewel in the crown in NASCAR's Winston Cup series of stock car races, the Daytona 500 is second only in status in the US to the Indianapolis 500. The high-speed Daytona showpiece is run in Florida on a similar 2½ mile (4km) banked circuit to Indianapolis and was first staged in 1959. And it was a clash between two of the all-time great Winston Cup heroes, Richard Petty and David Pearson, which provided the most sensational finish in the history of the race.

Petty – justifiably known as 'King Richard' – had won the Daytona 500 on five occasions since 1964. In 1975 he won a record 13 NASCAR victories on the way to his sixth Winston Cup title. He was now seeking the 178th victory of his career. Pearson (the 'Silver Fox') had 88 career wins to his credit, including success in the opening race of the 1976 season – the Winston Western 500 at Riverside, California.

Qualifying at Daytona was eventful enough in itself. A.J. Foyt went fastest in a Chevrolet, closely followed by Darrell Waltrip (Chevrolet) and Dave Marcis (Dodge), before all three were disqualified for various technical irregularities. Foyt and Waltrip were kicked out for having illegal fuel pressure assist systems and Marcis for a radiator block that was unstable at high speed. These disqualifications left a surprise all-Chevrolet front row of Ramo Stott – the only pole of his career – and Terry Ryan, who was making his

Winston Cup debut. Petty's STP Dodge was sixth on the grid and Pearson's red and cream Wood brothers' Purolator Mercury was seventh.

There had already been 33 official leadership changes before Pearson overtook defending champion Benny Parsons on lap 177 of the 200. Eleven laps later Petty seized the initiative but as he started the final lap, Pearson was right on his tail. Exiting Turn Two, Pearson moved towards the inside and when Petty drifted high along the back stretch, the wily Silver Fox was able to forge a car's length ahead approaching Turn Three. But, all too aware of the threat from behind, Pearson entered the turn too quickly and drifted high, allowing Petty to shoot through on the inside. As the pair came out of the last of the race's 800 turns, Petty held a lead of around 3ft (0.9m). At that point, Petty's car nudged Pearson's. The Dodge touched the outside wall and lurched at a crazy angle for a few yards before Petty managed to straighten it out. Meanwhile the impact had sent the Mercury spinning into the outside wall and on the rebound, its nose caught the rear of Petty's car, sending the King spinning head-on into the wall. It looked for a moment as if he was going to spin all the way to the finish but instead he slid to a halt on the infield grass, just 75 yards (68.6m) short of victory. Pearson's car was equally crippled but he succeeded in steering it across the grass and rejoined the track less than 10 yards (9.1m) from the finish, eventually crawling over the line at no more than 15mph (24.1km/h) for his only Daytona 500 success.

At the post-race inquest there was no hint of animosity between the two rivals. It was just one of those things. Pearson admitted that it was an unorthodox end to a race but added: 'If I'd backed across that finish line, it wouldn't have made any difference – as long as I was first!'

SIX WHEELS ON MY WAGON
SWEDISH GRAND PRIX, 13 JUNE 1976

One of the strangest sights ever seen in a Grand Prix was the six-wheeled Tyrrell Project 34, which competed in 1976 and 1977. Its four 10in (25.4cm) front wheels were designed to reduce drag and give improved cornering and braking due to the larger tyre 'contact patch'. In the hands of Jody Scheckter and Patrick Depailler, this motoring oddity proved surprisingly effective in its first season, its finest hour being at the Swedish Grand Prix at Anderstorp.

The brainchild of Tyrrell designer Derek Gardner, the P34 was not definitely earmarked for a Formula One future until the prototype showed such promise in testing against the standard car that race versions were hurriedly built. The car made its debut at the 1976 Spanish Grand Prix, but it was in Sweden that it came of age.

Scheckter, a winner at Anderstorp in 1974, caused a sensation by putting the Tyrrell on pole, but hopes of a famous victory were dashed when Mario Andretti made a flying start. Andretti proceeded to gain half a second per lap on the South African and it looked as though the Tyrrell was destined to finish no higher than runner-up. By lap 28 Andretti was leading by a comfortable nine seconds, but then it was announced that he had received a one-minute penalty for jumping the start. The penalty pushed him back to eleventh and although he fought his way up to sixth, he retired on lap 46 with an oil leak. Andretti's punishment left

Scheckter in command and he drove a steady race ahead of his team-mate. Depailler was pressed for a while by Chris Amon until the New Zealander went off in front of the stands. From fifth on the grid, the Ferrari of reigning champion Niki Lauda was unable to make any impression on the two Tyrrells and had to settle for third place, 12 seconds behind Depailler and 31 seconds behind winner Scheckter. Jacques Lafitte was fourth in a Ligier with James Hunt fifth in a McLaren.

Following this magnificent one-two, the Tyrrells continued to perform admirably throughout the season, Scheckter and Depailler finishing third and fourth respectively in the World Championship. Tyrrell continued with the experiment in 1977, when Ronnie Peterson replaced Scheckter, but the car was no longer as competitive, partly because tyre development for the smaller wheels was not as advanced as for conventional wheels. Consequently the concept was abandoned. March and Williams later tested cars with tandem rear wheels but neither actually raced, although the March did take part in hill climbs. Anyway in 1982 regulations restricted Formula One cars to four wheels. The six-wheeled revolution was over.

HUNT'S FLAG DAY

BRITISH GRAND PRIX, 18 JULY 1976

Feelings were running high in the build-up to the 1976 British Grand Prix courtesy of a simmering feud between Ferrari and McLaren which was about to boil over. The bad blood had started at the Spanish Grand Prix earlier in the season, when James Hunt's apparently victorious McLaren had been disqualified two hours after the race for exceeding the maximum allowable car width by 18mm ($^7/_{10}$in). The Ferrari number one, Niki Lauda, was awarded the race but two months later, on appeal, Hunt was reinstated as the winner. This controversial decision met with a frosty reception from Ferrari, not least because it cut Lauda's lead over Hunt in the World Drivers' Championship to 27 points – 52 to 25. The British Grand Prix at Brands Hatch was the next race on the calendar. This was the long, hot summer when the British public basked in unexpectedly high temperatures and found a new sporting hero in 28-year-old Hunt, the dashing blond bombshell with the film star looks and the aristocratic accent. Hunt had acquitted himself creditably with the Hesketh team over the previous three seasons but this was the year which really catapulted him into the big time. Lauda was his friend and great rival, so it was fitting that the pair lined up alongside each other on the front row at Brands as the season reached its halfway point. The second rank was made up of Mario Andretti's Lotus and Clay Regazzoni's Ferrari. Having qualified on pole, Lauda chose to start from the left side of the track, thereby avoiding the steep camber of the opening right-hander, Paddock Hill Bend.

Lauda got away well but Hunt missed a beat, enabling Regazzoni to fly past from the second row and attack his team-mate at Paddock. It was a bold but misguided assault, one which saw the two Ferraris touch wheels. Regazzoni spun, Hunt veered left to avoid him but hit the sliding Ferrari. The McLaren rode over the Ferrari's wheels and was launched into the air, crashing down to earth in an upright position but with the right front steering arm broken. In the midst of the mayhem Jacques Laffite crashed his Ligier into the bank. Hunt motored on slowly up the hill to Druids with one front wheel at a crazy angle and drifted down the other side towards Bottom Straight. He thought he was out of the race until he saw red flags indicating that proceedings had been stopped, so he turned off the track on to a little back road that led to the pits. As a crowd gathered around, Hunt climbed out and asked the mechanics to push the McLaren to the pit.

Half an hour later it was announced that the race would restart as if the first lap had not occurred, but that no car would be allowed to take part in the rerun if it had failed to complete the first lap. Additionally, no spare cars would be permitted to start. When the crowd heard that Hunt and, to a lesser extent, Regazzoni and Laffite, would be excluded, there was uproar. The McLaren spare car was wheeled on to the grid and as Hunt climbed into it, the bulk of the 77,000 crowd started to boo and whistle at the stewards. The slow handclap started up and some frustrated spectators threw beer cans on to the track. Hunt later remarked: 'It soon became clear that the organisers were going to allow me to start because if they didn't, they would have a riot on their hands!' In a miraculous change of heart, the stewards did indeed suddenly rule that Hunt could start after all because his car had been mobile when the race had been stopped.

And the issue of the spare car no longer applied since in the intervening period between the original crash and the restart, the McLaren mechanics had managed to repair the front suspension of Hunt's race car. So he got into that while Regazzoni and Laffite used their training cars.

In the restarted race Hunt sat behind Lauda for 45 of the 76 laps until he took the Austrian at Druids. With the Ferrari slowed by gear trouble, Hunt pulled away to win by a minute but even as he stood on the victory podium, moves were afoot to snatch away his moment of glory. Ferrari, Tyrrell and Copersucar all objected to Hunt's win on the grounds that his car hadn't technically been running when the original race was halted. Tyrrell and Copersucar subsequently withdrew their objections but Ferrari held firm.

Ferrari's appeal against the result was heard two months later. The McLaren hierarchy knew they were on to a loser when Lauda, having climbed out of his deathbed following his dreadful crash at the Nürburgring, was wheeled in by Ferrari swathed in bandages. Ferrari claimed that Hunt had abandoned his car, that the mechanics had pushed it with the race still in progress and that the McLaren would have been incapable of completing that first lap anyway. McLaren countered that Hunt had only stopped on seeing the red flag. Even though video evidence was produced to show that Hunt was still driving at the time, the FIA ruled that he hadn't actually been taking part in the race when it was stopped, and disqualified him. Lauda had won the sympathy vote, the general feeling being that Hunt's disqualification was to appease Ferrari following his reinstatement in Spain. It was a severe blow to Hunt's title aspirations. But the season was by no means over yet.

LAUDA
SURRENDERS THE TITLE

JAPANESE GRAND PRIX,
24 OCTOBER 1976

Niki Lauda's horrific crash at the Nürburgring on 1 August had changed the complexion of the Formula One season. In an incredible display of courage he was back behind the wheel 33 days later to finish fourth in the Italian Grand Prix, a performance which captured even the imagination of people with little or no interest in the sport. The Austrian's burnt face and singed eyelids became one of the year's enduring images, a symbol of heroism. To the neutral observer, nobody was more deserving of the World Drivers' Championship than Lauda, although victories for arch rival James Hunt in Canada and the United States had sliced the once seemingly unassailable lead to just three points approaching the final Grand Prix of the season at Mount Fuji.

Mario Andretti had qualified on pole in his Lotus with Hunt's McLaren alongside and Lauda on the second row. Come race day and the weather was appalling. *Motor Sport* wrote that 'streaming rain and low cloud swirled round the circuit and completely concealed Mount Fuji', restricting visibility to around 100 yards (91.4m). The track was frighteningly slippery for the untimed morning practice session. Just keeping the car on the road was a major achievement. Speed was very much a secondary consideration. The 73-lap race was due to start at 1.30p.m. but the drivers appeared to have little appetite for driving nearly 200 miles (322km) in such conditions. John Watson was heard to remark: 'In the wet, with no visibility, you only want someone in the bunch to lose control and you might have a massacre.' Of the 25 drivers, only the fearless Vittorio Brambilla (March) and Lauda's Ferrari team-mate Clay Regazzoni declared a definite commitment to start, although a few others indicated that they would probably be prepared to race if push came to shove. Hunt was among them. Ideally he wanted the race postponed but, rain or no rain, mist or no mist, he was not going to miss out on the chance of winning the World Championship. He had come too far ... and not only geographically. Lauda did not relish the prospect of racing at all. After Nürburgring he valued his life too much.

The inactivity around the pits made the 80,000 crowd restless and as it became apparent that no start was imminent, they started the slow handclap. The organisers shared the drivers' concerns but, in view of the crowd's reaction, feared that a cancellation might incite unrest and so they announced that the race would start at 3p.m. A number of the drivers still thought that conditions were too dangerous but their protests fell on deaf ears. Race officials insisted that the rain had stopped and that the worst of the water had been cleared from the track, despite the fact that pools of standing water remained on the pit straight. In the absence of solidarity, the drivers decided to give it a go. By three o'clock it was raining again, but the race went ahead and after a tentative warm-up lap through plumes of spray, the cars were away. Hunt got a flyer, slithering around the first lap from Watson's Penske. Back in third, Lauda was already struggling. Understandably beset with apprehension, the last straw came when he felt the Ferrari aquaplaning on the pit straight at the conclusion of the opening lap. 'It was absolutely unbearable,' he said later, 'sitting there panic-stricken, seeing nothing, just hunched down in the cockpit waiting for somebody to run into you.' After two laps, Lauda came into the pits and told the mechanics he was retiring from the race. Trying to protect their man, Ferrari subsequently explained away the retirement as a technical problem, but Lauda was honest and admitted that he had been too scared to continue. 'It was like murder out there,' he added. 'Sometimes I could not tell which direction the car was going. For me it was the limit. There are more important things in life than the World Championship.'

With Lauda's exit, Hunt needed only to finish fourth to dethrone the reigning champion and claim the crown for himself. All of the cars were on wet tyres but as the race progressed the rain began to ease off, with the result that the track slowly dried out. It was merely a matter of time before the drying surface began to destroy the wet tyres. Not that this appeared to concern Hunt who, approaching half-distance, held a comfortable lead over McLaren team-mate Jochen Mass. With Mass riding shotgun, Hunt's charge towards the title appeared unstoppable. Then on lap 36 Mass hit a wet patch and slid into the barrier, out of the race, thereby elevating the six-wheeled Tyrrell of Patrick Depailler to second. By now the sky overhead was blue. Mount Fuji was visible once again. The soft wet tyres were wearing away at an alarming rate. Hunt was in a dilemma. He could feel the left rear tyre deflating. Each time he flashed past the pits he looked for a sign telling him to come in for fresh tyres. Nothing. Depailler and Mario Andretti were starting to close. On lap 62 both overtook the ailing Englishman, but when Depailler pitted for new tyres, Hunt regained second spot.

His relief was short-lived. With six laps remaining his front left tyre disintegrated as he rounded the long loop to the start/finish straight. His only consolation was that the tyre had blown near to the pits, for it would not have lasted an entire lap. Hunt's pit stop lasted 27 seconds and dropped him back to fifth behind Andretti, Clay Regazzoni,

Alan Jones and Depailler. He rejoined the race in a blinding rage, convinced that his team's refusal to call him in earlier had cost him the championship. As he completed lap 69, a pit board mistakenly told him he was sixth. On lap 70 Hunt's fresh tyres enabled him to surge past Jones and Regazzoni, neither of whom had stopped. He was now third behind Andretti and Depailler, although he didn't know it at the time. Over the final two laps he desperately tried to catch Depailler but the Frenchman was still some 30 yards (27.4m) ahead at the chequered flag.

As he rose from his car, Hunt was in a black mood and began ranting at McLaren team boss Teddy Mayer for costing him the title. Having sorted out his calculations, Mayer tried to explain to his driver that he had finished third and was world champion, but Hunt couldn't hear a word through his helmet and carried on screaming abuse. Even when he removed his helmet, he still refused to accept the fact that he was champion until he had seen it in writing. There had been too many false dawns already in that memorable 1976 season.

FAN WORSHIP

SWEDISH GRAND PRIX, 17 JUNE 1978

Just as the 1976 Swedish Grand Prix had witnessed the sole triumph of the six-wheeled Tyrrell, so the same race two years later saw the only win of the infamous Brabham fan car. Indeed it was to be the car's solitary Grand Prix appearance, since fans were outlawed a few days after the race. But despite the controversy surrounding the innovation, Niki Lauda's victory at Anderstorp was allowed to stand and lives on today in the record books.

What was described as the most famous fan since Lady Windermere's was the creation of the Brabham team's South African designer, Gordon Murray. At the time, the 'ground effect' phenomenon was all the rage in motor-racing, ever since Colin Chapman had managed to harness under-car air pressure in his 1977 Lotus 78. Murray's response was to move the water radiator on the Brabham Alfa BT46 to a horizontal position above the engine and then to add a large tail-mounted fan at the rear of the car, the fan being driven by a shaft running from the gearbox. Murray also designed special skirts on the underside of the car so that the fan was able to suck air from beneath the car, like a vacuum cleaner. The result generated tremendous downforce, sucking the car closer to the ground.

The car tested successfully at Silverstone and Brands Hatch before being unleashed in Sweden. 'Movable aerodynamic devices' had been banned since 1969 so the fan's appearance stirred up considerable argument, and during practice both Emerson Fittipaldi and Mario Andretti complained bitterly that their visors were covered in dirt after following the Brabham. They maintained that any cars following the Brabham on the track would suffer as the stones and dirt sucked under it by the fan were thrown out behind. Nevertheless the fan was found to be within the rules, and Niki Lauda and John Watson responded by putting the BT46s second and third on the grid behind Andretti's all-conquering Lotus 79.

Watson made a poor start, but Lauda set off in pursuit of Andretti. After a couple of laps Watson was passed by the Arrows of Riccardo Patrese and then the second Lotus of Ronnie Peterson, which had been fourth on the grid, came in early for a tyre change and rejoined the race in eleventh. Seeking his first win of the season, Lauda swooped on the black and gold Lotus at half-distance and proceeded to pull away from Andretti with consummate ease. In a desperate attempt to claw back the ground, the Lotus eventually broke down. Behind, Alan Jones in a Williams was about to devour Patrese and move up to second when their wheels touched and Jones went off. Lauda went on to win much as he pleased by a commanding 34 seconds from Patrese, who held off Peterson by half a length at the finish. The fan car had given Brabham its first Formula One win for three years and Alfa Romeo engines their first victory since 1951.

Its success immediately prompted rival teams to attempt to develop their own system but before they had a chance to do so, the fans were declared illegal by the sport's governing body. However Lauda's victory was not taken away as, at the time of the race, the car had been perfectly legal.

Andretti and Lotus had the last word, going on to win the title, but they had been no match for the Brabham fan car on its one and only outing.

AN UNEXPECTED OBSTRUCTION

MONTE CARLO RALLY, JANUARY 1979

Since the very beginning of motor sport, French fans have earned an unwanted reputation for partisanship which occasionally borders on outright sabotage. Early motorcyclists from overseas found their chances of winning on French soil diminished greatly by the sudden appearance of tacks scattered across the road. The Monte Carlo Rally has long been a hotbed of dissent. Accusations of official bias against the British Minis were rife in the 1960s, but in 1979 it was the French spectators who were seemingly up to their old tricks, putting obstacles in the path of a Scandinavian victory and at the same time paving the way for a home triumph.

A total of 233 cars set off from nine European cities, the Common Route starting from Val le Bains. On arrival at Monte Carlo Hannu Mikkola in a works Ford Escort led Bjorn Waldegard's Escort RS by seven seconds with Walter Rohrl and Markku Alen, both in Fiats, a further 20 seconds adrift. France's Bernard Darniche, driving a Lancia Stratos, was back in sixth – 3min 7sec behind the leader. Divine intervention appeared to be his only hope of success.

Fifteen special stages followed, during which the Escorts pulled further away until Mikkola was handed a controversial five-minute penalty by the organisers for 'dangerous passing' on a public road near Digne. This action prompted dark mutterings of French bias. Waldegard was now 4min

7sec ahead of Alen and 6min 27sec ahead of Darniche. With the best 100 cars tackling the Mountain Circuit, Darniche set about clawing back the deficit, but his chances of overhauling the Swede still appeared remote.

On the final night there were ten stages, covering a total of 109 miles (175km). The first stage saw Darniche reduce the deficit by 22 seconds and on the first pass of the Col de Turini – where enthusiastic spectators tried to liven things up by shovelling snow off the banks on to the road – he pulled back another 42 seconds. With two stages remaining Darniche trailed by 1min 31sec, but then on that penultimate Villars stage, Waldegard, running first on the road, suddenly found his route blocked by two large boulders. He gamely tried to drive over them, but to no avail, whereupon his navigator, Hans Thorszelius, jumped out of the car, ran round to the front and levered them away. The delay cost Waldegard 25 seconds ... and the rally. For on the final stage Darniche was 21 seconds quicker than his rival to win by just six seconds overall. The French had lifted the Monte!

After five days and 2,500 miles (4,013km) of motoring, the rallying year's most prestigious event had been decided by a pair of judiciously placed rocks. Waldegard diplomatically preferred to attribute his defeat to the wrong choice of tyres over the closing stages, but others pointed the finger of suspicion firmly at French spectators whom they accused of positioning the boulders deliberately to scupper the Swede and engineer a home victory. The unsavoury incident left a nasty whiff hanging over the sport for several months.

THE RACE
THAT NEVER WAS
SPANISH GRAND PRIX, 1 JUNE 1980

The early 1980s were marked by an unseemly power struggle between motor racing's governing body, FISA (Fédération Internationale du Sport Automobile), and FOCA (Formula One Constructors' Association), which represented the interests of the British teams – which in 1980 meant everyone except Ferrari, Renault and Alfa Romeo. This latest row concerned the use of skirts on cars. These greatly increased downforce but could also be dangerous. If a skirt suddenly stopped functioning, which was liable to happen in the event of it being damaged by the car running over a kerb, the resultant loss of downforce could send the car spinning out of control. FISA wanted a ban on car skirts, but FOCA was determined to stand firm.

Already that season there had been skirmishes in Belgium and Monaco when FOCA drivers supported the stand their teams were making by refusing to attend the compulsory pre-race drivers' briefings. FISA president Jean-Marie Balestre's reaction to this outbreak of rebellion was to fine each offending driver $2,000.When the 15 drivers in question refused to pay the fines, their licences were withdrawn. This ugly stand-off came to a head shortly before the Spanish Grand Prix. Ferrari, Renault and Alfa Romeo remained loyal to FISA but the remaining teams demanded that the drivers' suspensions be lifted. FISA refused to back down and, with no solution in sight, pulled the Spanish Grand Prix from the World Championship schedule.

The prospects of the Grand Prix going ahead appeared remote but RACE (Royal Automobile Club Espagne), who owned the Jarama circuit north of Madrid and who organised the event, decided to defy FISA and take over direct control of the race from the international body. FOCA gave its backing so the Spanish Grand Prix went ahead, albeit without championship status and minus Ferrari, Renault and Alfa Romeo. With only 22 entrants, nobody could fail to qualify, as a result of which both Shadows made the starting line-up for the first time that year. But pole went to Jacques Laffite in a Ligier.

From fourth on the grid, Carlos Reutemann shot through to lead on the first of the 80 laps, followed by Laffite. Passing places were at a premium at Jarama – the only realistic overtaking spot being at the end of the main straight – and consequently Laffite found himself stuck behind Reutemann for longer than he anticipated. Then on lap 35 the pair came to lap one of the tail-enders, local driver Emilio Villota in a Williams. In attempting the manoeuvre, Reutemann and Laffite collided, putting both of them out of the race.

Nelson Piquet, who had been running third, now took the lead in his Brabham, only to retire on lap 47 with gearbox failure, thereby allowing Didier Pironi's Ligier into first place, pursued by Alan Jones in a Williams. With 14 laps to go Pironi lost a front wheel and Jones inherited a comfortable lead which he kept to the finish. Jochen Mass (Arrows) was second, ahead of Elio de Angelis (Lotus) and Jean-Pierre Jarier's Tyrrell.

Of course, Jones's victory counted for nothing and is excluded from the record books. To all intents and purposes, the 1980 Spanish Grand Prix never took place.

The next Grand Prix, the French, was due to be run on 29 June. That race – and indeed the remainder of the Formula

One season – was in jeopardy until five days beforehand when representatives of all the teams met in a London hotel and thrashed out an agreement. The skirts stayed – at least for the time being.

As for Jones, 'the race that never was' did no lasting damage to his title aspirations since he went on to win the championship anyway. Apart from the sport's reputation, the real loser was Patrick Gaillard who had finished sixth – and last – at Jarama in an Ensign. Denied a World Championship point, he never won another.

MANSELL:
A PAINFUL BEGINNING

AUSTRIAN GRAND PRIX,
17 AUGUST 1980

Forthright, demanding, paranoid and sometimes downright stubborn, Nigel Mansell has been described as a pain in the backside on more than one occasion. Whether or not he deserved that label, it was certainly applicable in a literal sense to his Formula One debut at the Österreichring in 1980.

Mansell came from the school of hard knocks. His was no overnight success story. He had served his apprenticeship in Formula Ford and Formula Three and was so determined to make it to the top that he accepted a Formula One test drive for Lotus even though he had a broken back at the time! Defying the pain, he showed enough speed on that test to persuade Colin Chapman to give him a chance. And so it was that Mansell came to line up in the 1980 Austrian Grand Prix.

Going into the race, Australian Alan Jones had a clear lead in the championship race courtesy of wins in Argentina, France and Britain. The Österreichring was the fastest circuit of the year (Spa being out of favour between 1970 and 1982) and in practice six drivers were fined a total of 30,000 Austrian schillings (about £11,000) for ignoring a red flag when Jochen Mass spun. René Arnoux put the turbo-engined Renault on pole, breaking his own lap record by a colossal five seconds, from team-mate Jean-Pierre Jabouille and Jones's Williams. Twenty-fourth and last on the grid was N. Mansell at the wheel of the exceedingly moderate Lotus-Cosworth 81B.

If Mansell thought things could only get better, he was mistaken ... sorely mistaken. A few minutes before the start the Lotus mechanics put the final touches to his car, including topping up the fuel tanks. Almost immediately he began to feel 'an intense burning pain in my backside and down my legs'. He realised that fuel had been spilt over him, whereupon the mechanics asked him whether he wanted to get out and live to race another day. But Mansell had waited so long for this opportunity that nothing was going to deny him, and he insisted on racing. In an effort to dilute the petrol, the crew tipped a bucket of cold water down the back of his seat. This had the desired effect for a while but after ten or so laps Mansell could feel the return of the burning sensation. The pain grew progressively worse. He likened it to being slashed with a knife. His agony lasted until lap 40 out of 54 when the engine of the Lotus blew up in sympathy. For the only time in his career, Mansell was relieved to be out of a race.

'The decision to race was the right one,' he said later. 'It showed I wasn't a quitter. But the problems started when I got out of the car and discovered that my hamstrings had shrunk where they'd been immersed in petrol for so long. Afterwards I had to have them stretched.' Scarcely able to walk, once home he went straight to hospital in Birmingham for treatment on the red raw blisters which covered his backside.

The race provided more pleasant memories for 37-year-old Parisian Jean-Pierre Jabouille who, after failing to finish in his previous nine Grands Prix, picked up only his second ever championship victory (he had won in France in 1979). Although team-mate Arnoux was the more fancied of the two Renault drivers, he was delayed by making three pit stops to rectify tyre trouble. This allowed Jabouille to build up a healthy ten-second lead over Jones, only to experience mechanical difficulties over the closing laps. Jones reduced the gap dramatically and at the final corner was right up behind the Frenchman, Jabouille hanging on to win by less than a second. Carlos Reutemann came third in the other Williams, while the unlucky Arnoux could finish only ninth despite breaking the lap record again towards the end.

Second place put Jones 11 points ahead of Nelson Piquet with four races to go, although the outspoken Australian was less than happy with his pit crew, claiming that they failed to keep him properly informed of the narrowing gap between himself and Jabouille. Had he known, he said, he might have been able to put on an extra spurt and snatch victory at the death.

Similarly for Mansell, it was not a race he would forget in a hurry. In fact for weeks to come he would be reminded of it every time he sat down.

THE LONG WAIT
INDIANAPOLIS 500, 24 MAY 1981

When Bobby Unser crossed the finish line eight seconds ahead of Mario Andretti for his third Indy 500 victory, little did he know that far from being the end of the race, it was really just the beginning. Sensationally disqualified the following day, Unser was eventually reinstated as the winner five months later after the longest and most contentious sequel to an Indianapolis 500.

Having put his Penske PC9 – the Norton Spirit – on pole, Indy legend Unser quickly had the first inkling that this was going to be no ordinary race. 'After the announcement of "Gentlemen, start your engines", smoke came from under the dash of my car, which told me my radio literally had gone up in smoke.' Deprived of the more advanced technological means of communication, Unser and team manager Roger Penske had to resort to basic finger signs – one for pit, two for wing, three for tyres. Unser also survived a hairy pit stop fire, choosing to drive his way out of it 'because those invisible flames have a tough time surviving at 200mph [321.8km/h]!'

The race developed into a fierce contest between Unser and the Wildcat-Cosworths of Mario Andretti and Gordon Johncock. When Johncock dropped out, Unser and Andretti remained locked in battle but the Penske, having led for most laps, held on to the finish to record a winning time of 3hr 35min 41.8sec. at an average speed of 139$\frac{1}{10}$mph

(223.8km/h). Unser was duly given the full Victory Lane treatment, bringing back memories of his two previous triumphs in 1968 and 1975.

Then came the sensation. Chief steward of the track Tom Binford stated that Unser had illegally passed ten cars while exiting the pit lane at a time when the yellow flags were out following a spate of accidents. The yellow flags created a 'hold station' period where overtaking was forbidden. Unser was penalised a lap for his misdemeanour. According to Binford, the second man home, Andretti, had only passed two cars in the same circumstances and so was promoted to first place. At the official victory banquet on the evening after the race, Andretti was declared the 'winner under protest'.

Unser launched an appeal and, after five months of investigation, he was reinstated as the winner of the 1981 Indianapolis 500. The appeal panel concluded that Binford's controversial penalty could only be imposed during a race. To illustrate their point, they used a basketball analogy where a game was concluded with a one-point margin of victory until the next day a foul was called, allowing the losing team to shoot uncontested free throws. These hypothetical throws were converted so that the losers became the winners. Obviously such a situation was no more acceptable in motor sport than it would be in basketball, and therefore Unser's appeal was upheld. The panel also determined that the rule in question had not been communicated clearly to any of the 33 drivers competing in the race.

Unser was fined $45,000, but the penalty was nothing compared to the rewards of winning a third Indy 500. And the verdict allowed Unser, one of the all-time great US drivers, to quit racing on a winning note before embarking on a new career as a TV commentator.

A FALLING-OUT
AMONG FRIENDS

SAN MARINO GRAND PRIX,
25 APRIL 1982

The 1982 San Marino Grand Prix was shrouded in controversy even before the start. Most of the British FOCA teams boycotted the event in protest at the disqualification of Nelson Piquet's Brabham and Keke Rosberg's Williams from the top two places in the Brazilian Grand Prix for brake water-cooling irregularities. As a result only 14 cars stood on the grid at Imola – Ferrari, Renault, Alfa Romeo, Tyrrell (who were only competing because they were sponsored by an Italian washing machine company), ATS, Osella and Toleman.

Despite the fanatical support of the home crowd, the Ferraris of Gilles Villeneuve and Didier Pironi were unable to compete with the Renaults driven by René Arnoux and Alain Prost. Arnoux took pole with Prost half a second slower. Villeneuve and Pironi were third and fourth on the grid, separated by 1.4 seconds, Pironi having survived a hairy high-speed accident during qualifying which saw him fly backwards into a barrier. There is no rule which says that team-mates have to get on – indeed most drivers regard their team-mate as their fiercest rival – but the Ferrari pair got on better than most. Both were highly talented drivers. Pironi was determined and resourceful while Villeneuve was fearless and flamboyant, a throwback to the likes of Nuvolari. Villeneuve was by nature a trusting guy, and he trusted Pironi. On the evening before the race the two men had dinner together with their wives. All was sweetness and light.

Come the off and Arnoux was first away, pursued by Prost, but the latter was passed by the two Ferraris before the end of the opening lap, and when Prost retired with piston failure on lap seven, the leading three were the only serious contenders. The trio were separated by less than a second when, on lap 44 out of 60, Arnoux was forced to retire, his car belching out smoke. This left the Ferraris to win as they pleased, the only threat, apart from some unforeseen mechanical problem, being fuel consumption, since Imola was the thirstiest circuit in Formula One. Villeneuve now assumed the mantle of leader. Eager to conserve fuel, he eased off for a few laps and did not worry when Pironi passed him. The French-Canadian soon regained first place. To the crowd, the pair were simply putting on a show to liven up what might otherwise have turned into a dreary procession.

However, the Ferrari pit, which was without team leader Mauro Forghieri (absent on family business), became concerned that this constant jousting was drinking up the fuel, of which there was only just enough to see them through to the finish even at normal levels of consumption. So they ordered Villeneuve to slow, and he immediately responded by easing off to the tune of two seconds per lap. Ferrari team orders were that the man ahead when the red cars became first and second (in this case Villeneuve) should be the man ahead at the finish. Villeneuve clearly understood that and, backing off as ordered, was not unduly perturbed when Pironi put on a sudden spurt to overtake him again seven laps from the finish. This time the lead was not so easy to retake. On lap 58, Villeneuve drew alongside his team-mate under braking at the right-hander known as Tosa, only to be unceremoniously cut off. But on the following lap, Pironi did let him past. As far as Villeneuve was concerned, that was that. Pironi's antics had been nothing more than showmanship and now the pair would cruise around for a stress-free one-two. Then as they headed down towards Tosa for the last time at a conservative 180mph (289.7km/h), Pironi suddenly shot past on the approach to the corner, catching Villeneuve totally unawares. The two cars nearly touched. Since that was the last overtaking point on the track, there was no opportunity for Villeneuve to retaliate, and it was Pironi who crossed the line the winner of the 1982 San Marino Grand Prix.

Pironi stood on the victory rostrum waving happily to the crowd but next to him Villeneuve had a face like thunder. He didn't want to be there at all and had to be persuaded by his wife to appear before the Imola fans. As soon as the ceremony was over, Villeneuve stormed away from the circuit without saying a word to Pironi. In Villeneuve's opinion, Pironi had stolen the race in an act of treachery. Pironi pleaded his innocence and expressed the hope that he hadn't upset his team-mate, but Villeneuve did not appear interested in platitudes. He told reporters: 'The first two or three times he came inside and passed, I thought, well, he wants to play a little bit, and I never defended myself. But him, he was just racing, and I was too stupid to realise it. I thought he was an honest guy ...'

They never did make up. Villeneuve was killed while practising for the next Grand Prix at Zolder in Belgium. Some say his mind was still on Imola.

ALL CHANGE AT MONACO
MONACO GRAND PRIX, 23 MAY 1982

The fortieth running of the Monaco Grand Prix provided arguably the most dramatic ending to a race since the inauguration of the World Drivers' Championship, as a combination of light rain and spilt oil turned the circuit into a skating rink over the closing laps.

Until then the race had been pretty much a procession with championship leader Alain Prost taking the lead on the fifteenth of the 76 laps after his Renault team-mate René Arnoux had dropped out with mechanical failure. Riccardo Patrese in an old Brabham-Ford was tagging along in second but Nelson Piquet in the new, but still unreliable, turbo Brabham BMW had been forced to retire after 50 laps. The main excitement had centred on the battle for fourth place where Keke Rosberg (Williams) pressed Andrea de Cesaris (Alfa Romeo), until the Finn called it a day on lap 64 with a damaged front suspension.

Then a race which had appeared to be drifting towards a quiet conclusion suddenly came alive when it started to rain with five laps remaining. The first casualty was Derek Daly's Williams, which slid into the barrier at Tabac when lying fifth. Despite losing a rear wing and damaging the gearbox, Daly managed to get going again and was far enough ahead of Elio de Angelis's Lotus to retain his place, but then the battered Williams seized up completely at Rascasse hairpin and Daly was out of the race. Up front,

Prost still had a seven-second lead over Patrese and seemed secure until on lap 74 the Renault slid sideways exiting the seafront chicane, hit the barriers and lost a wheel. This put Patrese into the lead but less than a minute later he, too, slid to a halt near Loews hairpin. Didier Pironi's Ferrari and de Cesaris both got through before Patrese was able to get moving once more.

Patrese began the final lap a distant third with seemingly no hope of victory, unaware that ahead of him both Pironi and de Cesaris were reduced to cruising because the punishing track had left them short of fuel. Pironi ground to a halt in the tunnel, out of fuel and with an electrical problem to boot. Seconds later, on the approach to the tunnel, de Cesaris ran out of fuel. Patrese could hardly believe his eyes as he passed the two stationary cars and proceeded to tiptoe to the finish for his first-ever Grand Prix win. Pironi and de Cesaris were credited with second and third places respectively a lap behind the winner, with Nigel Mansell a hard-earned fourth in the Lotus.

A HINT OF
NATIONAL BIAS?

SWISS GRAND PRIX, 29 AUGUST 1982

It could probably only happen in France. A French driver is
leading with two laps remaining but is being rapidly caught
by a Finn. So what does the man with the chequered flag do?
He tries to wave it two laps early to secure a home victory.

Such a scenario might sound far-fetched, but few neutrals
who were present at Dijon in August 1982 could come up
with any other explanation for the curious antics at the end
of the Swiss Grand Prix.

It was an odd race from the outset. But then again, it was
an odd year all round in Formula One. For the answer to
the riddle, 'When is a Swiss Grand Prix not a Swiss Grand
Prix?' is simply, 'When it was in 1982.' Already that season
the Spanish Grand Prix had not taken place, a race had
suddenly appeared around the streets of Detroit, the Dutch
Grand Prix had happened when everyone thought it would
be off, there were four Grands Prix in five weeks when it had
been universally agreed to allow two weeks between races,
and, to cap it all, there were now two Grands Prix in France.
The official French Grand Prix had taken place earlier in
the season at Paul Ricard, but now a second event – calling
itself the Swiss Grand Prix even though it was being staged
on French soil – cropped up at Dijon. It was all highly
confusing. Alain Prost put his Renault on pole from team-
mate René Arnoux and Riccardo Patrese in a Brabham-
BMW. But there was little jubilation in the Renault camp as

Arnoux had just announced that he was joining Ferrari for the 1983 season. Renault had no intention of keeping him anyway – not after he had disobeyed team orders to snatch the prize from Prost at the official French Grand Prix – but the atmosphere in the pit was one of stony silence whenever Arnoux was around, not least because Renault were anxious to prevent him giving away precious team secrets to the opposition.

Patrick Tambay withdrew on the morning of the race with back trouble, leaving 25 starters. Arnoux got away fastest and led them around for the first time but then Prost took control. Nelson Piquet's Brabham-BMW went second, only to surrender the position to Arnoux when stopping for fuel and tyres at mid-distance. In fact Piquet's pit stop proved a disaster for the Brazilian as his replacement tyres were out of balance. He was lapped soon after rejoining the race and never again threatened the leaders.

Piquet's decline allowed Keke Rosberg to inherit third place in his Williams but a delay in lapping Andrea de Cesaris, who refused to let him by, meant that his chances of catching the two Renaults appeared remote. Then with ten of the 80 laps remaining, Arnoux retired, the car's fuel injection system having failed. And suddenly Prost was slowing too. He had lost fourth gear. As Rosberg pegged him back, the French crowd grew increasingly uneasy. With just over two laps remaining, it seemed only a matter of time before Rosberg caught and passed the Renault. At that point Williams team manager Peter Collins noticed that the official with the chequered flag was about to hang it out … two laps early. Collins quickly pointed out the 'error' and the flag was put away. Sure enough on lap 79, to the accompaniment of groans from the crowd, Rosberg caught and passed Prost at the downhill left-hander. The Frenchman had no answer.

After seconds that year in Brazil, the United States, Belgium and Austria, Rosberg approached the finish line for the eightieth time and prepared to celebrate his first ever World Championship Grand Prix win – at the forty-ninth attempt. Yet bizarrely, having tried to end the race two laps prematurely, the man with the chequered flag now compounded his blunder by failing to spot Rosberg as he roared by. So the bemused Finn did an extra circuit and finally received the flag at the end of lap 81! In mitigation, it was pointed out that the Swiss had not staged a Grand Prix since 1954 ...

Niki Lauda came third for McLaren while Nigel Mansell, having started from last on the grid, fought his way up to finish eighth of the 16 survivors. Rosberg's sole victory of the year turned out to be sufficient to clinch the title, but no thanks to the man with the chequered flag at Dijon ... whether his actions were guided by sheer incompetence or something more sinister.

IT'S A WASHOUT
BIRMINGHAM SUPER PRIX,
25 AUGUST 1986

As far back as 1960, a group of motor sport enthusiasts proposed turning Birmingham into Britain's answer to Monte Carlo. Perhaps because Gas Street Basin did not quite possess the allure of the French Riviera, this attempt to stage Britain's first street race came to nothing. But the idea was revived from time to time, and in the late 1970s and early '80s permission was granted for a series of parades of old racing cars to be held in the city. These proved such an attraction that the plan for a Birmingham street race reared its head once more, but this time with the backing of the local council. It was a period of high unemployment in the West Midlands and the city council was anxious to improve Birmingham's rather dour image, to make it more attractive to investors and tourists. After a local referendum offered overwhelming support for the idea of staging a Grand Prix on the dual carriageways in the city centre, an Act of Parliament gave the official go-ahead. Public roads were to be closed over a two-day period around the 1986 August Bank Holiday. The Birmingham Super Prix was up and running.

A 2½ mile (4km), L-shaped circuit was mapped out around the inner ring road and adjoining thoroughfares, making it the fastest street circuit in the world. Sir Jack Brabham, who had business interests in the Midlands, voiced his approval of the event and the city council forked out £1.5

million in anticipation of attracting 100,000 spectators over the two days. Temporary grandstands were built and 8 miles (12.9km) of crash barriers and wire fences were erected to protect people and houses. The main race was announced as the 52-lap Halfords Super Prix – a round of the European Formula 3000 Championship, just one step below Formula One. Its inclusion was significant. For the ultimate goal was to bring the British Grand Prix itself to Birmingham.

Inevitably, not everyone in Birmingham welcomed motor racing to the city streets. Local church leaders decided to cancel some Sunday services because they thought the noise would make worship impossible and residents close to the circuit were made virtual prisoners in their own homes, a feeling intensified by the eight-foot-high wire fences which had suddenly appeared at the end of their small front gardens. Some were horrified at the prospect of trying to eat Sunday lunch while racing cars sped by at 150mph (241.4km/h) barely 10 yards (9.1m) from their dining-room windows.

Despite a delay to the start of practice after vandals had removed bolts from crash barriers, Sunday passed off smoothly. The spectator numbers were high – their behaviour guaranteed by the presence of around 1,000 police officers – and the standard of racing was first rate. Monday's big race, the Super Prix, was therefore eagerly anticipated.

But the British summer rarely fails to disappoint. No matter that thousands of would-be spectators had pre-booked, that the event was being televised in 35 countries, or that a city's sporting reputation was at stake: the heavens opened. And the more it rained, the more people stayed away, the police estimating that only 20,000 braved the elements on that Bank Holiday Monday. The prolonged and torrential downpour reduced the streets of hope to a river of broken dreams. The signs were ominous when driver Robin Smith was taken to hospital in a Thundersports race after his Ford-Cosworth had hit crash barriers at over 100mph (160.9km/h) and burst into flames, but the organisers were determined that the main course on the sumptuous menu should proceed. Thus the Super Prix began, only to disintegrate into a series of high-speed crashes on the slippery circuit. Finally, with two cars strewn across the road after 25 highly eventful laps, the decision was taken to abandon the race. Victory – of sorts – went to Luis Sala in an F3000 Ralt-Cosworth, but many drivers were critical of the organisers for not stopping the race earlier.

Although faced with a loss of £400,000 on the event, John Charlton, chairman of Birmingham City Council's Road Race Committee, remained upbeat: 'I am amazed we have been able to pull it off when everybody said that we could not. We have produced one of the best road race circuits in the world and we are guaranteed to hold it until 1990. We don't do things by halves in Birmingham. We have bid for the Olympics in 1992 and we can bid for the Grand Prix. We want to make Birmingham the sporting capital of Britain.'

The world awaits.

A FAMILY AFFAIR
DAYTONA 500, 14 FEBRUARY 1988

The thirtieth anniversary Daytona 500 provided an appropriate story when father and son Bobby and Davey Allison finished first and second for a unique Valentine's Day family double.

At 50, Bobby Allison was a seasoned campaigner at Daytona with two previous wins there to his name, the first back in 1978. Davey was 26 and had already earned a reputation as a very fast racer. That is precisely the attribute needed for Daytona where, in 1988, Ken Schrader put a Chevrolet Monte Carlo on pole at a speed of 193⅖mph (311.9km/h) – and even that was 15mph (24.1km/h) down on the previous year following the introduction of new regulations which reduced the cars' power by 150bhp. Schrader's Chevrolet team-mate, Darrell Waltrip (his car painted in the livery of Tide washing powder), started fourth on the grid of 42 but led the field for the first ten laps. He was followed by Rusty Wallace in a Pontiac, Bobby Allison in a Buick Regal and Davey Allison in a Ford Thunderbird. On lap 11 Bobby Allison moved into the lead, using the slipstream of the car ahead, but two laps later Waltrip pulled off a similar manoeuvre to retake first place and was followed through by Davey Allison.

On lap 32 Mark Martin's Ford blew its engine, bringing out the yellow flags. The drivers headed for the pits and when racing resumed Wallace found himself in the lead.

Then on lap 53 Bobby Allison seized the initiative once more and this time began to pull away from the chasing pack, before Waltrip, despite being handicapped by extra-curricular pit stops, fought his way back into contention. A major incident occurred on lap 103 when Richard Petty lost control of his Pontiac coming out of a turn and was shunted by Phil Barkdoll's Ford Thunderbird into the path of A.J. Foyt's Oldsmobile Delta. Petty's car somersaulted through the air in spectacular fashion and smashed against the safety fence, sending pieces of debris flying in all directions. What remained of the car finished up in the middle of the track, necessitating another session of racing under yellow flags. Remarkably Petty escaped with nothing more serious than an ankle injury.

By lap 153 Waltrip had forced his way back into the lead from Davey Allison with father Bobby in third, but another crash led to more yellow flags and a further change in the order. After that final round of pit stops, Davey Allison led away from Waltrip and Bobby Allison, only for Waltrip's challenge to fade thanks to a blown cylinder. This left father and son to battle it out to the death, and Bobby's experience prevailed when he overtook the Ford to come home the winner by just two car lengths. His time was 3hr 38min and his average speed for the race a cool 137½mph (221.3km/h).

Afterwards the oldest-ever winner of the Daytona 500 was congratulated by his wife Judy, who joked: 'He'll probably be here till he's 95!' Bobby gushed: 'It's just a special feeling. I saw the nose of his car coming out of the corner of my eye, and I thought I had the suds to beat him. He is a tremendous competitor. It's a great feeling to see somebody you think is the best coming up in the sport and know it's your son.' Davey was equally complimentary. 'I've had dreams for a long time about battling down to the wire with my dad. The only difference was that I never had dreams of finishing second. The whole race I was trying to put myself in a position where I was going to win the race and, hopefully, Dad would finish second. My whole concentration was on winning. If my car could have beaten him, it would have. I didn't think of him as my dad until the chequered flag fell. But really, it's better than if I had won myself – he's always been my hero.'

However, it was not all happy families. In June that year Bobby Allison was involved in a horrific smash at Pocono, Pennsylvania, which put him in hospital for three months with fractured bones and serious internal injuries. He never raced again. As a result of the smash, he suffered memory loss and had no recollection of his third Daytona victory. Luckily his son was on hand to tell him all about it.

Three years later the Andretti family – Mario, his sons Michael and Jeff, and his nephew John – became the first four family members to start the Indianapolis 500. Michael finished second, John fifth, Mario seventh and Jeff fifteenth. Also in 1991 the Andrettis filled the first three places at the Milwaukee Mile, Michael winning from John and Mario. Jeff let the side down by only finishing eleventh.

THE BATTLE OF SUZUKA

JAPANESE GRAND PRIX,
21 OCTOBER 1990

To say that there was no love lost between Ayrton Senna and
Alain Prost is like saying that Britain and Germany didn't
get along terribly well between 1939 and 1945. Although
they were McLaren team-mates for a while, they were poles
apart. Senna was the wild, hot-headed Brazilian, capable of
moments of genius and moments of madness. Prost was
the analytical – sometimes aloof – Frenchman, nicknamed
'the Professor'. Both were great drivers, but both thought
they were king of the road.

The presence of two such strong personalities in the
same team may have looked good on paper but in practice
it was little short of a nightmare. It was similar to having
an orchestra with two conductors, and neither was happy
to play second fiddle. The tension between the pair first
surfaced at the 1988 Portuguese Grand Prix when Senna
ruthlessly chopped Prost at 190mph (305.8km/h) as the
Frenchman tried to pass. Senna took the title that year, but
in 1989 Prost was ahead on points as the season entered
its penultimate round in Japan. Prost needed only to finish
in front of Senna to become champion for the third time.
Ominously, he issued an advance warning that he was not
prepared to tolerate any of the Brazilian's rough-house
tactics on this occasion. He would fight fire with fire. Prost
led from the start but Senna, in a typically determined
drive, gradually pegged back the advantage. With ten

laps remaining the cars were running nose to tail, Senna desperately searching for a hint of an opening. Six laps from the finish he thought he had found one – up the inside at the chicane. He left the braking as late as he dared and dived for the gap. Prost simply turned in on him and took both cars out of the race. Prost was champion. Each blamed the other for the collision.

For the 1990 season Prost had joined Ferrari. Again the Japanese Grand Prix at Suzuka was the penultimate round but this time the positions were reversed. With only five wins to Senna's six, Prost had to score at least one more point than Senna to keep the title battle alive going into the final race at Adelaide. More significantly, as it transpired, if neither car finished at Suzuka, Senna would be champion. Senna put the McLaren on pole with Prost alongside him, just three-tenths of a second behind. It had all the makings of a charge into the first corner. Whoever got there first would have an outstanding chance of staying there. Senna knew that, and was furious at being ordered to start from the right-hand side of the track, which was much dustier than the left. Having gained pole, he thought he had earned the right to decide where he would prefer to start from. He protested, but FISA president Jean-Marie Balestre refused to reconsider. Senna simmered and sulked. In his eyes, Prost, although only second fastest, had been given the side of the track with the superior grip. Senna made a mental note of his race plan: 'If Prost gets the best start, then I'm warning him, he'd better not turn in on me because he isn't going to make it.' It was to prove a chillingly accurate prophecy.

Race day was warm and sunny, a deceptively tranquil backdrop to the drama that was about to unfold. On the front row of the grid, the two combatants sat in their cars a matter of yards apart, waiting anxiously for the green light. When it finally came, Prost, as Senna had feared, got the better start from the cleaner side of the track. Prost, with a slight advantage, inched towards the racing line which he would need to negotiate Turn One, the Ferrari's superior power giving him a lead of almost a car's length approaching the corner. Instead of coming across and blocking Senna completely, Prost edged back a fraction towards the outside. Senna sensed a gap, albeit a minimal one, and made for it. Prost eased off slightly to take the turn but Senna kept his foot hard down and smashed into the Ferrari, taking both cars out of the race. Mission accomplished. Senna was champion.

Prost was outraged. 'I am not prepared to fight against irresponsible people who are not afraid to die,' he stormed. Senna maintained the pretence of innocence ... at least for another year. But in the meantime the shortest championship decider in history had gone his way. Sure, it was controversial, but in Senna's book the ends always justified the means.

THE 25-MINUTE GRAND PRIX

AUSTRALIAN GRAND PRIX, 3 NOVEMBER 1991

Ayrton Senna had already sealed the 1991 Formula One World Drivers' Championship by the time the cars headed for Adelaide for the last event of the season. It was to be one of the shortest races in living memory.

It was run in torrential rain with visibility down to the bare minimum. Many of the leading drivers, including rain-master Senna and Nigel Mansell, felt that the race should never have started, even though Mansell's Williams team still had a chance of lifting the constructors' championship at the expense of McLaren.

From the start, Mansell tucked in behind Senna's McLaren. Mansell said it was like groping in the pitch dark: 'I followed Ayrton round and gauged my driving by listening to his engine, to his gear changes. Then I would do the same, hoping I hadn't misheard his car. But as far as seeing is concerned, forget it.' Soon a number of cars went off on the hazardous back straight and while the marshals frantically waved yellow flags (to indicate no overtaking), the rescue services were busily lifting battered cars off the circuit. At one point Mansell poked out from behind Senna to have a look and found himself heading straight for a marshal's car!

Mansell was expecting to see the red flag signifying the end of the race after only four laps but the organisers kept the drivers out there for another ten circuits. Indeed the race was only finally stopped when Mansell spun off and crashed into a concrete wall, an accident which left him with a badly swollen ankle. As soon as Mansell went off, Senna started gesticulating angrily for the race to be stopped, and the stewards took the hint. Only 14 of the scheduled 81 laps had been completed but, despite the atrocious conditions, the clerk of the course was eager to give the rain a chance to ease off and kept everyone waiting for another 50 minutes before finally calling it a day. The placings were calculated on the last completed lap, which put Mansell second behind Senna despite his spin. Gerhard Berger was third in the other McLaren, a result which gave the team its fourth constructors' championship in a row. Since there had barely been 25 minutes' actual racing, half points were awarded to the first six drivers.

The curtailed race was unsatisfactory for all concerned, not least FISA vice-president Bernie Ecclestone who was

highly critical of the marshalling and stewarding. He did not share the view that conditions were unraceable and thought that producing a white flag (to indicate there was a slow car on the circuit) together with yellow flags to stop any overtaking, would have given the rescue crews time to clear the debris. Senna, Mansell and co. were just happy to be back in the dry.

MANSELL AND
THE SAFETY TRUCK
INDY CAR CHAMPIONSHIP ROUND 6,
13 JUNE 1993

Piqued by the signing of Alain Prost for the Williams team for 1993 and by the fact that Frank Williams was not willing to meet his pay demands, reigning Formula One world champion Nigel Mansell packed his bags and took his ample frame across the Atlantic to go Indy Car racing for Paul Newman's team. Many doubters thought he was taking one hell of a gamble simply to prove a point, but it turned out to be a gloriously successful year, with Mansell taking the United States by storm and powering his way to the Indy Car championship to become the first person ever to lift the two titles in successive years. Indeed for one week, before Alain Prost snatched the Formula One crown at Estoril, Mansell was in the unique position of being a dual champion, holding both titles simultaneously.

Inevitably the triumphal march was interrupted by the occasional hiccup. One was in Detroit.

The city had been synonymous with indifferent racing since 1982 when it first staged the United States Grand Prix, the potholed street circuit and uninspiring layout falling foul of the Formula One drivers. Alain Prost intimated that he would rather retire than have to race there every week and Keke Rosberg described it as dull. 'Most of the stuff,' said the Finn in 1985, 'is 90 degrees around the block, 50 yards [45.7m] and then another 90 degrees. I just can't get excited about it.' In 1989 the Detroit track became part of the Indy Car season. The following year's race was stopped when Mario Andretti smashed into one of the organisers' safety trucks, and then Mario's son, Michael, ploughed into his father. So it was by popular request that in 1992 the race switched to the city's tricky 2¹⁄₁₀ mile (3.4km) Belle Isle Park circuit on the Detroit River. Here, too, there was to be no shortage of incident, especially when Mansell came to town in 1993.

After five weeks of racing on ovals, a twisting street course with 14 turns made a pleasant change for the Indy Car drivers, although it made little difference to the composition of the grid with Mansell, the clear championship leader, taking his familiar pole position in the Newman-Haas Lola-Ford ahead of the Penske Racing cars of Emerson Fittipaldi and 24-year-old Canadian Paul Tracy. Already that season Mansell had shown a tendency to throw away his hard-earned pole with sluggish starts and this looked to be no exception when, at the fall of the green flag, he was seen shaking his fist in frustration as Fittipaldi surged past him on the run to Turn One on the first of the 77 laps.

Mansell was clearly unhappy with the Brazilian's lightning getaway and 13 laps later Championship Auto Racing Team (CART) officials decided to give a stop-go penalty to Fittipaldi for jumping the start. This decision was met with disbelief in many circles, since the general rule was that once the green flag dropped, the race was on. If Fittipaldi had been moving forward at the start, it was up to the starter not to display the green flag. 'If there's something wrong with the start, they should throw the yellow,' said an irate Roger Penske. 'They threw the green and we went. What happened after that doesn't mean a thing.'

To add insult to injury, Fittipaldi crashed while trying to make up the lost ground and team-mate Tracy, who had been running second, was penalised for speeding on the pit road. But Mansell was not about to get off lightly either. First, he collided with Stefan Johansson while the pair were disputing third place and then – the ultimate ignominy – he crashed out of the race while swerving to avoid a safety truck!

Having started from tenth on the grid, 1988 Indy Car series winner Danny Sullivan now found himself narrowly in the lead from Galles Racing team-mate Al Unser Jr. Although Sullivan was slowed by a leaky turbo, Unser was unable to force his way past on the winding circuit. Increasingly frustrated, Unser made a desperate move with nine laps remaining but Sullivan refused to yield and forced his team-mate into the cones. Having penalised drivers in practice and qualifying for hitting the cones, CART steward Wally Dallenbach felt duty bound to be consistent and issued Unser with a stop-go penalty. Sullivan held on to win from Brazilian Raul Boesel, with Mario Andretti third. A disgusted Unser was back in sixth. His only consolation was that for once he had a better day at the races than Mansell.

THE RACE AGAINST THE TRAIN

ORIENT EXPRESS RACE, 9 SEPTEMBER 1993

Inspired by tales of derring-do from the 1920s when the famous Bentley Boys raced the Blue Train between London and the French Riviera, sipping champagne en route, the 96 Motoring Club organised a 1,000 mile (1,609km) race against the Orient Express from London to Milan.

So it was that 45 classic cars – among them a D-Type Jaguar, a Mércedes gullwing, a Daimler SP250 sports car, and a 1922 Vauxhall – lined up at London's Victoria Station one Thursday alongside the Orient Express. As the train pulled away from the station, Lord Montagu of Beaulieu waved off the cars on their journey across five countries, which included a crossing of the Swiss Alps. The rules of the race were simple: any car taking a short cut or exceeding that country's speed limit would be disqualified. Michael Scott of the 96 Motoring Club emphasised: 'Any car that arrives in Milan before 5p.m. on Friday evening (the tenth) will obviously have speeded and will be disqualified.'

After racing around Brands Hatch and the Monthléry circuit outside Paris, the cars completed their first day with a lap of the Nürburgring, near Frankfurt. The second day, racing against the train resumed with a dawn start from Frankfurt. Although the drivers stopped off for the obligatory sip of champagne, the result was never in doubt, most of the cars arriving in Italy hours before the Orient Express. The first to reach Milan – eight hours in advance of the train – was Mark Chauveau in a 1973 Maserati, but he admitted that he had cheated by missing out Germany in order to fulfil an important lunch date in the Italian city. 'It was such a complicated route,' he said, 'that I decided to go via Geneva in search of some entertainment. I don't think I can be classified as a winner, but I had great fun. In Italy I was mobbed at every traffic light as the Italians went crazy over the car.'

Ultimately Pentti Airikkala was declared the winner in a Mitsubishi 3000 GT. His scariest moment was arriving in Milan and not being able to find the railway station. He resorted to flagging down a young moped rider who led him to the station. As the organisers summed up: 'The train was thrashed.'

LET THE SUNSHINE IN
WORLD SOLAR CHALLENGE,
27 OCTOBER 1996

Held every three years and run over a 1,870 mile (3,009km) course from Darwin to Adelaide, the World Solar Challenge has earned a reputation as the world's biggest race for solar-powered transport. The 1996 event attracted no fewer than 57 cars and bicycles with the British hoping to improve on their dismal showing of previous years. Only one British competitor, Philip Farrand, an engineer with the Williams Grand Prix team, had ever even managed to complete the distance, coming second in the conventional lead-acid class in 1993. In that same year the only other British entrant, laboratory engineer Brian Hamilton, failed to make it off the start line.

But the British faced tough opposition from the Honda 'Dream' car which, with its covering of mono-crystal silicon cells, was capable of speeds in excess of 90mph (144.8km/h) and could cruise at 56mph (90.1km/h). The energy from the solar panels was stored in a silver-oxide zinc battery powering a DC brushless motor. In the world of solar transport, it was a formidable machine.

The starters – scaled down from an original list of some 300 – set off from Darwin on 27 October for their long trek across the outback via Alice Springs to the south. The race was spread over four days, but there was rarely any doubt as to which car would be first to reach Adelaide. The Honda Dream car won in 33hr 32min at an average of 55¾mph

(89.8km/h), clipping over two hours off the previous record. A team of Swiss students were runners-up with their Schooler Spirit '96 car in a time of 35hr and Japan's Aisol III finished third in 37hr 18min. For the British, world solar supremacy remained a distant vision.

ROAD RAGE

EUROPEAN GRAND PRIX, 26 OCTOBER 1997

Ever since Michael Schumacher took Damon Hill out of the 1994 Australian Grand Prix to clinch the World Drivers' Championship, accusing fingers were pointed in the German's direction. Schumacher maintained that the Adelaide incident was simply a racing accident, but many – Hill included – suspected a more sinister motive. Schumacher's ability as a driver was not open to question, but few doubted his ruthlessness either. It seemed that, faced with the prospect of losing the title, he would not hesitate to remove his rival from the equation. He had done it once and got away with it, argued the cynics. If a similar situation arose in the future, would he be able to resist doing the same again? The answer came three years later in the European Grand Prix at Jerez in Spain. If you're a Schumacher fan, look away now.

This time Schumacher's chief rival was the young Canadian driver Jacques Villeneuve in a Williams. It had been a close-fought contest all season but after 13 rounds of the 17-race championship, Schumacher, now with Ferrari, held a ten-point lead. He was within sight of becoming the first Ferrari driver since Jody Scheckter in 1979 to win the world title, and he knew how much that meant to the Ferrari fans, the famous *tifosi*. But then Villeneuve retaliated with wins in the Austrian and Luxembourg Grands Prix before Schumacher countered with victory in Japan. Going into the final race at Jerez, Schumacher led by a solitary point. If neither car finished, he would be world champion.

Mindful of this, at the pre-race briefing Formula One supremo Bernie Ecclestone told all the drivers that he wanted a fair fight on the track. 'If one or other of the drivers takes the other out,' he warned, 'then the punishment will be draconian.' The stage was set in qualifying when Villeneuve, Schumacher and Heinz-Harald Frentzen (Williams) all recorded identical times. Since Villeneuve was the first to set the time, it was he who started from pole, alongside Schumacher. The German was philosophical, pointing out that it was the start that mattered. And the next day it was Schumacher who made the dream start, roaring away from the two Williams to the delight of the 18,000 *tifosi* watching the race on a giant screen in the town square at Maranello. Villeneuve's slow getaway left him in third, but on lap eight Frentzen pulled over to let his team-mate pass and launch a full-scale attack on Schumacher.

For the time being, Schumacher, in the supposedly inferior car, was able to hold Villeneuve at bay and had extended his lead to 5.2 seconds when the first round of pit stops began. With new tyres, a frustrated Schumacher exited the pits, only to find himself stuck behind Frentzen and David Coulthard, enabling Villeneuve to close right up. When Frentzen and Coulthard pitted, Schumacher had a clear run and on lap 30 it was the Canadian's turn to suffer as he lost precious ground trying to lap Norberto Fontana's Sauber. By the time Villeneuve eventually got past, he was 3.2 seconds behind Schumacher. After the two leaders had made their second stops, Villeneuve was noticeably closer … close enough to attempt the bold passing manoeuvre which would ultimately decide the race and the championship.

Schumacher was leading Villeneuve along the back straight on lap 48 out of 69. Approaching the right-hander known as Curva Dry Sac, Villeneuve attacked Schumacher from a long way back, taking him completely by surprise. Diving through on the inside – into a gap which Schumacher had surprisingly left – Villeneuve braked extremely late and was able to draw level with the Ferrari. At the last minute, Schumacher suddenly jerked the steering wheel and drove into the side of the Williams. It was the same story as at Adelaide, but this time with a different ending. For while Schumacher finished up on the gravel and out of the race, Villeneuve's car, although damaged, was able to continue. The biter had been bitten.

Villeneuve nursed his car around the remaining 21 laps. At first he wasn't sure whether it would hold out but after two slow laps, he saw that the suspension was bearing up and felt confident enough to push on again. Then towards the finish, not needing a victory, he allowed the McLarens of Mika Hakkinen and Coulthard to pass, the Finn going on for his first Grand Prix win at the ninety-sixth attempt. The four points which Villeneuve secured for finishing third made him world champion.

At the post-race inquest into the drama on lap 48, Villeneuve was remarkably diplomatic. 'I was aware that Michael could take me out. In fact, I think the move only had a 50 per cent chance of success. But I had noticed that my car was definitely better after I fitted new tyres and I could not wait to attack. It would have been pointless to finish second and I preferred taking the risk of finishing in the gravel than to stay behind until the end.'

Schumacher once again protested his innocence. 'He tried a rather optimistic attack. It worked for him but not for me. I am human and, unfortunately, make mistakes. I do not make many, but this was a big one. I see no reason to apologise.'

His old adversary Damon Hill was predictably critical, maintaining: 'Michael showed his true colours and got what he deserved.' What Schumacher also got was the threatened 'draconian punishment' which saw him stripped of his second place in the World Championship. Few outside Germany or Maranello had much sympathy for him.

AFTER YOU, MIKA!
AUSTRALIAN GRAND PRIX,
8 MARCH 1998

Just over four months after Jacques Villeneuve had gifted him the European Grand Prix, Mika Hakkinen received another present – this time from his McLaren team-mate David Coulthard in the form of the 1998 season's opening race, the Australian Grand Prix. Whereas Villeneuve's gesture was motivated by self-preservation, plus the fact that the McLarens were going faster than him anyway, and consequently scarcely caused a ripple on the Formula One millpond, Coulthard's unprecedented act of generosity was a different matter altogether. At Albert Park, Melbourne, he handed over a winning position to a team-mate whom he clearly had the beating of on the day. Puzzled observers reckoned that it was a move the mild-mannered Scot would live to regret. How right they were.

The winter testing programme strongly suggested that McLaren would be the team to beat for 1998. The two drivers were full of confidence, to the extent that they made a pre-race pact whereby whichever of them was ahead entering the first corner would be allowed to stay there for the rest of the Grand Prix, barring mishaps. The idea behind the agreement was that it would stop the two team-mates from fighting – and possibly destroying – each other. Nevertheless it was a curious state of affairs for modern motor racing and one which led directly to the controversy which subsequently engulfed the 1998 Australian Grand Prix.

McLaren threw down the gauntlet in qualifying, Hakkinen and Coulthard posting the fastest times by over 0.7 seconds from Michael Schumacher's Ferrari and the Williams of reigning champion Jacques Villeneuve. That may not sound much in ordinary terms, but in the supercharged world of Formula One where technology is king, 0.7 seconds could seem like an eternity.

Coulthard later joked that when he agreed to the pact, he had naturally assumed that he would be leading into the first corner, but in fact the opposite was the case. With the cars held for a long time on the grid under the red lights, Coulthard's engine started to smoke. At the split second he glanced down, the lights went out. The momentary hesitation allowed Hakkinen to get away first and lead his team-mate through that all-important opening turn. Once safely in front, the McLarens set a blistering pace. Schumacher tried to hang on to Coulthard's coat tails but on lap six out of 58 he retired with engine trouble. Even at such an early stage, he was the sixth retirement, following in the wake of both Stewarts and his brother Ralf. Nor could Villeneuve stay with the McLarens and soon he was passed by Williams team-mate Heinz-Harald Frentzen, the Ferrari of Eddie Irvine and the Benetton of Giancarlo Fisichella.

With the McLarens apparently coasting to victory, a bizarre incident occurred on lap 36. Hakkinen was just about to lap Irvine when he heard indistinct noises over the radio. He thought he had to come in and refuel and since he was level with the pit lane entry, he dived in before checking on the radio. But when he reached the McLaren pit, there was nobody around, so he simply drove straight on and rejoined the race! However, the detour had dropped him back to second spot, some 13 seconds behind Coulthard.

Eight laps later the McLaren pit informed Coulthard over the radio that Hakkinen had lost the lead because of a misunderstanding. Remembering the pre-race pact, Coulthard thought long and hard about what to do. He said afterwards: 'It was a very difficult decision to take. But I was alone in front without any pressure, which allowed me to think about it calmly and to reach the decision that this was Mika's race by right.' Accordingly, he told the pit that he was going to let Hakkinen through. Thus, three laps from the end of what had otherwise been a keenly contested race, the Albert Park crowd and millions of television viewers across the world were treated to the strange – and somewhat unsatisfactory – sight of the leader slowing down and moving aside to allow his team-mate to pass.

Hakkinen went on to record a hollow victory from Coulthard, Frentzen, Irvine, Villeneuve, and the Sauber of Johnny Herbert. Of course when he crossed the finish line, only the McLaren team knew about the private agreement, but even when it became public knowledge there was widespread incredulity. How could Coulthard afford to give the man who was likely be his principal championship rival a four-point start? The answer was: he couldn't.

At the post-race press conference Hakkinen was asked whether he would do the same for Coulthard if the boot was on the other foot. There was a seemingly interminable pause before Hakkinen grinned: 'Yes, yes, of course.' Three years later, when Hakkinen announced his retirement from F1, Coulthard was still waiting.

SCHUMACHER WINS IN THE PITS

BRITISH GRAND PRIX, 12 JULY 1998

A rain-soaked British Grand Prix at Silverstone ended in mayhem with nobody seeming to know whether Michael Schumacher or Mika Hakkinen had won. It all centred on the interpretation, delivery and timing of a ten-second penalty to Schumacher but when the fuss had died down, it emerged that the German had earned the distinction of becoming the first driver ever to win a Grand Prix in the pit lane.

After a lightning start to the season when they looked destined to sweep all before them, the wheels had come off the McLaren wagon over the previous two Grands Prix. Comprehensive defeats in Canada and France – coupled with two Schumacher successes – had put a different complexion on the championship race. After eight rounds, Schumacher was within six points of Hakkinen with Coulthard – perhaps beginning to regret his largesse in Australia – languishing 14 points behind the German in third. Suddenly there was a real race on. Ferrari could sniff McLaren blood and their drivers, especially the outspoken Eddie Irvine, were making plenty of capital out of the Woking team's sudden vulnerability. But now McLaren were back on home soil. The British Grand Prix would be the perfect venue to answer their critics.

Hakkinen did his bit, qualifying on pole, but Coulthard was only fourth fastest – behind Schumacher and Jacques

Villeneuve. Irvine and Heinz-Harald Frentzen made up row three. Hakkinen was cautiously optimistic but the weather forecast for Sunday's race was heavy rain, and Schumacher was the acknowledged rain-master.

Hakkinen and Schumacher both made good starts but Villeneuve was away slowly and found himself behind Coulthard and the Sauber of Jean Alesi, who gained four places from his grid position. Irvine also made a poor start and things looked grim for Ferrari when Coulthard eased past Schumacher at Abbey Curve. After a dozen laps light rain began to fall and when it became increasingly persistent, the cars started a mad scramble for the pits. Some didn't make it in time. To the dismay of the crowd, Damon Hill spun off on lap 14 and was followed two laps later by Frentzen. Only Hakkinen of the leading bunch moved on to wet tyres, the rest opting for intermediates. Coulthard made steady inroads into his team-mate's advantage until the rain suddenly started to get heavier around lap 26. Soon Johnny Herbert and Mika Salo (Arrows) went off and Esteban Tuero's Minardi was involved in a shunt with Ricardo Rosset's Tyrrell. Coulthard, in particular, was struggling in the wet conditions and spun three times in quick succession, finally exiting the race on lap 38. He later expressed his anger at being put on intermediates while Hakkinen had the benefit of wets.

The rain had now reached monsoon level, resulting in further casualties including Rubens Barrichello (Stewart), Olivier Panis (Prost) and Pedro Diniz (Arrows). Even Hakkinen went off on to the grass at Bridge Corner but managed to keep going. Conditions were so treacherous that the yellow flags were brought out, but while lapping the Benetton of Alexander Wurz, Schumacher failed to spot the flags and passed the Austrian. Moments later the safety car appeared. In an instant Hakkinen saw his 38-second lead over Schumacher reduced to nothing. To make matters worse, the McLaren had not emerged unscathed from its excursion on to the grass, although Hakkinen was unsure as to the extent of the damage. Six laps later the rain had eased sufficiently for the safety car to withdraw. Almost immediately Hakkinen went off at Becketts and Schumacher swept through into the lead.

But behind the scenes there was high drama. Schumacher had been awarded a ten-second penalty for passing Wurz under the yellow flags, but the Silverstone stewards took 31 minutes to notify Ferrari of the decision when the rules state that it should be delivered within 25 minutes of the offending incident. Moreover, the piece of paper handed to Ferrari sporting director Jean Todt was, at best, ambiguous and, at worst, illegible. Ferrari were unsure whether it was a stop-go penalty, which would necessitate Schumacher coming into the pits for ten seconds before rejoining the race, or if the ten seconds was simply to be added to his final time. In the absence of any clarification from the stewards, Ferrari let Schumacher continue on his way and then brought him in for the penalty at the end of the final lap, by which time he had a 20-second lead over Hakkinen. So at the end of the sixtieth and last lap, Schumacher came into the Ferrari pit, which was beyond the finish line, and served his ten-second penalty, this being added to his overall time. He thus won the British Grand Prix while stationary.

Not that any of the soaked crowd had any idea who had won at that point, for it was some time before it filtered through that Schumacher had officially been declared the winner. McLaren protested, arguing that as the yellow flag incident had occurred 12 laps before the finish the transgressor was supposed to sit out the ten seconds in the pit in a stop-go penalty rather than have them added to his time. However, the protest was rejected since the delay was deemed to be the fault of the stewards rather than Ferrari.

So Schumacher kept the race. Hakkinen's championship lead was down to two points. Game on.

CARNAGE AT LA SOURCE
BELGIAN GRAND PRIX, 30 AUGUST 1998

The 1998 Formula One season had already experienced more than its fair share of drama, but the Belgian Grand Prix was something else: a first corner pile-up involving 13 cars, an explosive confrontation between Michael Schumacher and David Coulthard and, at the end of it all, Jordan's first Grand Prix win at the 127th attempt. Who says motor racing is dull? Since Silverstone, Mika Hakkinen had notched back-to-back wins in Austria and Germany and, although Schumacher rallied with victory in Hungary, the Finn held a seven-point lead coming to round 13 at Spa. After Jacques Villeneuve had emerged unharmed from a 186mph (299.3km/h) practice crash – 'the best accident I've had in Formula One so far', he joked – qualifying gave little hint of the excitement to come. Hakkinen and Coulthard put the super-fast McLarens on the front row of the grid for the third successive race and the ninth time in all that season. But the happiest man was Damon Hill who, following two fourth-place finishes in the last two races (his first points of the year), conjured up extra speed from the Jordan to go third fastest, ahead of Schumacher, Eddie Irvine and Villeneuve. Hill was ecstatic, declaring the qualifying performance to be almost as good as a race win. 'At the start of the season our car was a disaster,' he said, 'and now we have completely turned the situation around.'

If qualifying had been a triumph for McLaren, the start of

the actual race was anything but. Hakkinen got away best in the wet to lead into La Source hairpin from Villeneuve and Schumacher, but behind them Coulthard and Irvine touched, causing the McLaren to hit the wall of the old pits and rebound into the middle of the track. With visibility reduced considerably by the spray, the cars behind had no chance of taking evasive action. Car upon car crashed into one another, the track quickly becoming littered with red, white, silver and blue wreckage. As wheels bounced in slow motion down the hill towards Eau Rouge, the race was stopped. Fortunately the mass collision had occurred at the slowest point on the circuit, with the result that none of the drivers suffered anything more serious than bruising.

The cars were not so lucky. No fewer than 13 of the 22 starters were involved – Coulthard, Irvine, Johnny Herbert (Sauber), Alexander Wurz (Benetton), Shinji Nakano (Minardi), the Tyrrells of Ricardo Rosset and Tora Takagi, the Prosts of Olivier Panis and Jarno Trulli, the Arrows of Pedro Diniz and Mika Salo, and the Stewarts of Rubens Barrichello and Jos Verstappen. Since their teams only had one spare car, Panis, Barrichello, Salo and Rosset were unable to take part in the restart, leaving just 18 hoping for better luck next time around.

Following a 50-minute delay for the track to be cleared, they set off once more. Hill got a flier, leaving the McLarens and the Ferraris in his wake as they rounded La Source. This time it was Hakkinen's McLaren that didn't make it, clipping Schumacher on the exit from the hairpin and sliding along the track before being shunted by Herbert. Both Hakkinen and Herbert were out of the race. McLaren misery was compounded 30 seconds later when Coulthard had a coming-together with Wurz and dropped back to the rear of the field. The safety car came out for one lap while Hakkinen's broken car was towed away, and this enabled Coulthard to make up a little of the lost ground.

By lap five out of 44 the rain was getting heavier and

Schumacher used his expertise in wet conditions to sweep past Hill into the lead. Elsewhere the slippery surface was taking its toll. Tagaki spun out of the race on lap 11, Villeneuve on lap 17 and Irvine from third place on lap 26. Schumacher now had a 37-second advantage over Hill. Victory – and with it, the lead in the championship – appeared a mere formality.

Then Schumacher came up to lap Coulthard, who slowed on the straight to allow the Ferrari to pass. But through the clouds of spray, Schumacher failed to detect Coulthard's reduction in speed and ploughed into the back of him. The front wheel of the Ferrari was ripped off and both cars limped back to the pits where Schumacher had no choice but to retire. In a blind fury, he headed straight for the McLaren garage where he had to be restrained by mechanics of both teams from hitting Coulthard, whom he blamed unreservedly for the accident. Schumacher even went so far as to suggest that it was deliberate. 'He slowed down at a point where we are normally flat out,' raged Schumacher. 'I was not expecting it at all. David has enough experience to know that in this rain there was no way I would realise he was slowing down and have enough time to react.' Coulthard, who accused Schumacher of behaving 'like an animal' when he stormed into the McLaren pit, argued: 'My engineer told me over the radio to let Michael through, so I stuck to the right-hand side of the track. All I know is he drove into me. What was I supposed to do? I cannot drive looking behind me all the time. It was not my responsibility to watch him. It was up to him to be careful.'

Meanwhile, in what was almost a carbon copy incident, Giancarlo Fisichella failed to spot Nakano's Minardi through the rain and spray and slammed into it. The safety car made another appearance while the remains of the Benetton were cleared from the track. When the safety car turned off, there were only 12 laps left and, with the field bunched up, Hill was just ahead of team-mate Ralf

Schumacher and the Sauber of Jean Alesi. Ralf immediately tried to attack Hill at the next corner, only to be warned off by the Jordan team. The orders from the team were that Hill was to win the race. So for the remaining laps, Ralf sat frustrated in second place. It had not been a good day for the Schumacher family.

But for Damon Hill, Eddie Jordan and all those who watched this remarkable race unfold, it had been a day to remember.

THE SHED, THE BED AND THE BOOT

DONINGTON PARK WACKY RACES, 28 AUGUST 1999

In the summer of 1997 the *Sun* newspaper came up with the idea of staging an alternative British Grand Prix for bizarre customised vehicles. But what started out as a spoof has developed into a proper race, held annually at Donington Park's August Bank Holiday meeting.

The 1999 event was so popular that it had to be divided into two classes – road-going and non-road-going. The second category attracted no fewer than ten entries, including a motorised garden shed, a four-poster bed, a roller boot, a sofa, a giant orange, and a toilet and bath combination.

The shed was the brainchild of Derbyshire farmer George Shields, who originally built it in 1997 as a practical joke for a friend's wedding. 'I couldn't find the pony and trap he wanted,' said Shields, 'so I decided to make some transport of my own. My friend thought his stag party had finished the night before. Little did he know he was going to show up at the church in a garden shed!' The Shields machine, which held the distinction of being the only garden building ever to have completed the journey from John O'Groats to Land's End under its own steam, consisted of a quad bike engine underneath and a six-by-four garden shed on top, complete with five hanging baskets. It had a top speed of 55mph (88.5km/h) and did 50 miles (80.5km) to the gallon. 'Where to put the exhaust pipe was a bit of a problem,' he admitted, 'but I got it to go out of the door. The whole conversion is really comfortable, with a big cushion on the seat. It's very noisy and smelly to drive, but that's OK because there is a television and radio inside. And it doesn't like corners much – especially at 55mph.'

Race organiser Edd China had three entries – the sofa, the toilet and bath, and the four-poster bed. The bed, welded to a 1,600cc Volkswagen Beetle engine, was inspired by the 1960s TV series *The Monkees*. 'Their show would start with them pushing a bed around town,' said China. 'I just thought I wanted to live my life like that. It cost £5,000 and took two months to build, but it's a car that impresses the women.'

The toilet and bath combination was driven by 65-year-old Donington Park track marshal Frank Richardson. 'It is terrible to drive,' he confessed, 'although once you get it up to 40mph (64.4km/h) it tends to straighten itself out.' Richardson had a nasty moment during practice when clothes from the laundry basket on the front became entangled with one of the wheels.

At the wheel of the giant rollerskate, a promotional vehicle for Derby Rollerworld, was the firm's general manager Terry Wilcox. Other entrants included Mick Pike in a dodgem car, Geoff Quaife in the Outspan Orange, and Mike Hand driving a stuffed horse and covered wagon, in which the indicators were in the horse's eyes. Among those sadly missing for the 1999 event was a motorised skip.

It may not have been the full Grand Prix distance but a few laps of Donington Park still produced plenty of excitement. In the end victory went to the dodgem car from the Outspan Orange, which just pipped the bed. The shed broke down. The non-road-going class resulted in a win for a customised fire engine, beating an armchair and a gondola on wheels.

NO TYRES FOR IRVINE
EUROPEAN GRAND PRIX,
26 SEPTEMBER 1999

The 1999 World Championship season had been turned on its head following Michael Schumacher's broken leg at the British Grand Prix. The Silverstone race left Schumacher's Ferrari team-mate Eddie Irvine eight points behind championship leader Mika Hakkinen, but victories in the next two races – in Austria and Germany – had propelled the Ulsterman into pole position. Hakkinen fought back with a win in Hungary and a second in Belgium but missed out at Monza where Irvine, too, could only finish sixth. Going into the European Grand Prix at the Nürburgring, with just two more races to follow, the two chief protagonists were level on points. Irvine was relishing his new-found, albeit temporary, status as Ferrari number one while Hakkinen, judging from the way he broke down in tears at Monza after spinning off while comfortably in the lead, was definitely starting to feel the pressure. With Schumacher's legions of German fans rooting for Irvine, the Nürburgring appeared the ideal place to increase that pressure, yet in the heat of battle it was Ferrari that buckled.

The European Grand Prix was a race which had everything – tension, farce, joy, despair, drama, anger, and at one stage seemingly a new leader every lap. There was enough excitement for half a dozen Grands Prix.

As is so often the case in Formula One, the overriding factor was the weather. The morning rain had stopped before the end of the Saturday lunchtime qualifying session but the track remained wet and the best times were set in the closing minutes, with Heinz-Harald Frentzen's Jordan snatching pole from David Coulthard and Hakkinen. Irvine could manage no better than ninth. He would be starting from a long way back. The track was dry for start time but the overcast sky suggested that it was unlikely to remain so for the full 66 laps. An aborted start, after Minardi driver Marc Gene had signalled a problem on the grid, was an indication of the drama that was to follow almost from the moment the lights went out. As the field flowed into the first corner, Damon Hill's Jordan lost power and Alexander Wurz had to swerve to avoid it. In doing so, he clipped Pedro Diniz's Sauber which flipped over on to the grass. The safety car was called out while Diniz was extricated, happily with nothing more serious than a few bruises. When the safety car departed, Frentzen led from Hakkinen, Coulthard, Ralf Schumacher and Giancarlo Fisichella. By lap 17 Irvine had worked his way up to fifth. At that point it started to rain.

Three laps later Hakkinen, in second, pitted for wet tyres. This proved a grave misjudgement, as the shower soon passed and he found himself losing up to ten seconds per lap. But his move seemed to spread panic. On lap 21 the Ferrari pit were getting ready to bring Irvine in for new tyres when Mika Salo (Schumacher's replacement in the Ferrari team) came in unexpectedly, needing a new nose-cone and tyres. He was away again after a 30-second stop, but the unscheduled visit had caused his tyres to become mixed up with those of his team-mate. To complicate matters further, Irvine and Ferrari technical director Ross Brawn, seeing the rain easing off, hastily switched their choice of tyres from wet to dry, forcing the mechanics to shelve one set of tyres and find another four. Irvine wanted to stay out for an extra lap to give the mechanics time to prepare, but he didn't have sufficient fuel and so he had to come in just 23 seconds after Salo had left. As the Ferrari crew scrambled for Irvine's fresh set of tyres, they could find only three. The right rear tyre was still in the garage. This Keystone Cop performance cost Irvine a pit stop of 28.2 seconds – 20 seconds over the norm – and dropped him out of the points-scoring positions. It was an unmitigated disaster.

Irvine's only consolation was that Hakkinen had fallen back to tenth on the unsuitable wets, but on lap 24 the Finn tried again, this time calling in for dry tyres.

Eight laps later, the first and second-placed drivers, Frentzen and Coulthard, pitted together. Frentzen got away first but the Jordan ground to a halt with an electrical problem at the very next corner, handing Coulthard the lead. By lap 38 it had started to rain heavily again. Coulthard, on dry tyres, was slipping and sliding his way around the track but was hanging on to his ten-second lead over Ralf Schumacher until he pressed too hard and slithered into the gravel and out of the race.

This presented the younger Schumacher with a 20-second advantage over Fisichella, but Schumacher was on a two-stop strategy and when he pitted on lap 44, the Benetton driver became the new leader. But four laps later Fisichella, like Coulthard before him, failed to cope with the wet track and spun out of the race. Presented with the lead once more, Schumacher was prevented from taking advantage when, on the following lap, he suffered a right rear puncture and limped to the pits. With Schumacher down to fifth, Johnny Herbert, who had started a lowly fourteenth on the grid, suddenly found that it was his turn to lead.

Greatly assisted by a switch to wets on lap 35, Herbert kept his head while all around were losing theirs. Having previously finished just four races that season, the popular Englishman held on for his third Grand Prix win and, more importantly, the Stewart team's maiden victory. And with team-mate Rubens Barrichello finishing third behind Jarno Trulli's Prost, it was a highly emotional day for Jackie Stewart and his colleagues. There was joy, too, for Minardi.

Luca Badoer seemed set to pick up the Italian team's first points for four years, only for his car to die on lap 54 when he was lying fourth. All was not lost, however, as teammate Gene came through to finish sixth and earn Minardi a priceless point. But it was another hard luck story for former world champion Jacques Villeneuve, still seeking BAR's first point. He was poised for fifth place when his clutch failed.

Villeneuve's loss proved Hakkinen's gain. Having appeared to give up, Hakkinen found a new lease of life towards the end and, four laps from the finish, harassed Irvine into a costly mistake. Once past Irvine, Hakkinen profited from Villeneuve's late exit to finish fifth and pick up two vital points. Irvine ended up seventh to round off a hugely disappointing day for Ferrari.

Irvine was understandably angry at the prolonged pit stop. 'It is a problem when you have one team of mechanics serving two cars,' he said. 'We should have two teams doing it. We screwed it up.' Ferrari president Luca di Montezemolo was even more scathing. 'Ferrari's fans are rightfully very upset and we cannot tolerate it. We made a complete mess of it and it must never happen again.'

THE SIX-DAY
WORLD CHAMPION
MALAYSIAN GRAND PRIX,
17 OCTOBER 1999

The penultimate round of the 1999 season, the inaugural Malaysian Grand Prix will long be remembered for Michael Schumacher's dramatic return from injury and for a Ferrari disqualification which saw Mika Hakkinen crowned world champion for six days.

Going into the race, Hakkinen was two points ahead of Eddie Irvine thanks to the Ferrari fiasco at the European Grand Prix. But now Irvine was able to welcome back team-mate Schumacher following a six-race absence. Schumacher himself had no chance of the title but Irvine and Ferrari were hoping that he would be able to protect the Irishman from the two McLarens. The question was, would Schumacher really be prepared to help Irvine win the title, thereby depriving himself of the glory of bringing that long-awaited World Championship to Ferrari? The cynics suggested that Schumacher would prefer to walk barefoot over burning coals than assist Irvine. They were to be proved wrong.

The pre-race noises were less than encouraging, however. A week before the showdown at Sepang, Schumacher was still expressing doubts about being ready to return to competitive driving, but a sudden change of heart (perhaps accompanied by a little arm-twisting from Ferrari) saw him make an emotional comeback. In qualifying he drove as if he had never been away, putting the car on pole, ahead of

Irvine and the two McLarens. It was clearly going to be a race of tactics with each team trying to outmanoeuvre the other. For Ferrari, Ross Brawn committed Schumacher to one stop in order to allow Irvine to build up the gap he needed for two stops. The idea was for Schumacher to ride shotgun for Irvine, keeping the chasing McLarens at bay. It was a role he was to play to perfection. For their part, McLaren deployed Coulthard to hustle and harry Irvine in the early stages and accordingly the Scot began with a lighter fuel load than usual.

Schumacher made a perfect start and led away from Irvine, Coulthard and Hakkinen. As early as the fourth lap, Schumacher ushered Irvine through into the lead and then set about holding off the McLarens. But a lap later Coulthard caught Schumacher napping at the first chicane and dived into second place. For the next nine laps Coulthard pursued Irvine with a vengeance before the McLaren's fuel pressure fell and he was forced to retire.

Hakkinen now had to take on the Ferraris single-handed. Try as he might, he could not get past Schumacher, who used a variety of contentious blocking tactics to keep the Finn at bay while Irvine disappeared into the distance. When Irvine pitted for the second time, Schumacher, on his one-stop strategy, was in the lead but, obeying team orders, he duly waved his team-mate through once more. At the end of the 58 laps, it was Irvine who picked up the ten crucial points, with Schumacher second and Hakkinen, never able to break free from the red menace, picking up just four points for third place.

Hakkinen was not happy and accused Schumacher of repeatedly accelerating and braking to hold him back. McLaren team boss Ron Dennis moaned: 'Such tactics might be within the regulations, but it is not sporting. If that is the way you want to go about winning the championship, then fine. It's consistent with Ferrari's style.'

Then a few hours after the race had ended, while

Ferrari celebrated and McLaren licked their wounds, the sensational news came through that both Ferraris had been disqualified by the stewards because the cars' air deflectors were found to be 10mm (⅖₁₀in) under the regulation width. Hakkinen was promoted from third to first, making him the 1999 world champion.

Hakkinen was still unhappy – that wasn't how he wanted to win the title. Ferrari appealed, pointing out that the offending deflectors had been used at the European Grand Prix and on all three days in Malaysia. Nobody had queried them before. To lose the championship over such a tiny miscalculation seemed harsh in the extreme. The appeal was heard in Paris at the end of the week. Ferrari were reinstated. The 1999 season would go to the wire.

As it turned out, the Japanese Grand Prix was something of an anti-climax. Hakkinen won in a canter, Irvine unable to manage any better than third. Hakkinen was once again crowned world champion – and this time it was for longer than six days.

COULTHARD AND THE TRESPASSER

GERMAN GRAND PRIX, 30 JULY 2000

Most employees unhappy at the manner of their dismissal seek recourse through the law. Unfortunately a 47-year-old Frenchman chose to register his protest by wandering on to a race track in the middle of a Grand Prix. Miraculously his reckless behaviour did not result in an accident, but it did cause lasting damage to David Coulthard's hopes of becoming world champion.

With victories at Melbourne, Interlagos, Imola, the Nürburgring and Montreal, Michael Schumacher looked to have all but sewn up the championship by the middle of June. Then a retirement at Magny-Cours and a first-corner exit at the A1-Ring left the door open for McLaren, Schumacher's lead over Coulthard being cut to just six points prior to his home Grand Prix at Hockenheim.

In a wet qualifying session, Coulthard underlined his growing confidence by taking pole from Schumacher, Giancarlo Fisichella's Benetton and Mika Hakkinen. Schumacher's Ferrari team-mate, Rubens Barrichello, started back in eighteenth place from where it seemed that he would be unable to offer much help to the championship leader.

All year, the McLaren team had been unhappy with Schumacher's tactic of pulling across at the start. He had cut across Coulthard at both Imola and Magny-Cours, forcing the Scot to lift. Here, it was payback time. As the lights went out, Coulthard pulled across to the inside line to block Schumacher, who reacted immediately by switching to the outside. In doing so, he drove straight into Fisichella's front wing and the pair slid off into the tyre wall – the second race in a row where these two had failed to make it around the first corner. The man to profit from this chaotic start was Hakkinen, who led at the end of the first lap from Coulthard and Jarno Trulli (Jordan), while further back Barrichello had shot up to eighth. The Brazilian soon forced his way up to third before a pit stop on lap 17 out of 45 made it clear that he was on a two-stop strategy, whereas the McLarens were intending to stop just once.

Hakkinen continued to lead Coulthard around until a bizarre incident took place on lap 24. A spectator burst through the fences, ran across the track near the Clark Kurve and began walking along the grass verge. It later transpired that he was protesting against his dismissal from Mercedes-Benz. While the race organisers waited for security guards to remove the man, the safety car was brought out. Coulthard had been due to pit on that lap but when he saw Hakkinen dart into the pits, he stayed out, unaware that the safety car was lying in wait. Stuck behind the safety car, poor Coulthard had to suffer a slow lap before he could get to the pits, eventually rejoining in sixth. The anti-Mercedes protester had cost a McLaren-Mercedes driver his chance of the race.

The safety car stayed out for three laps, during which time 14 cars pitted. Hakkinen retained his lead, from Trulli and Barrichello, but then on lap 29 the safety car was introduced again after the Sauber of Pedro Diniz slammed into the back of Jean Alesi, scattering wheels and bits of chassis from the Prost over the track. With 13 laps remaining, it started to rain heavily in the stadium section of the circuit, but not in the forest, placing the drivers in a dilemma. Eleven of the 15 cars still running pitted to go on wets, including leader Hakkinen, but Barrichello opted to stay out on drys. This propelled Barrichello into the lead and, driving with great skill on the slippery surface, he held on to win by seven seconds from the fast-closing Hakkinen, with Coulthard in third and Jenson Button in fourth just missing out on his first podium.

For Barrichello and Ferrari, it was a moment to savour – his first Grand Prix win in his 124th start. For Coulthard and McLaren, it was the one that got away through no fault of their own. As McLaren's Ron Dennis caustically commented: 'We had flexibility in our strategy, but not sufficient to accommodate a deranged spectator who wandered on to the circuit costing us the race and endangering his and the lives of the drivers.'

THE UGLY SIX PACK
UNITED STATES GRAND PRIX,
19 JUNE 2005

The relationship between Formula One and the American public had always been a fragile one. A number of fleeting attempts had been made to woo America in the past but deep down its heart really lay with NASCAR. With F1 chief Bernie Ecclestone producing a bigger bunch of flowers, America finally agreed to enter into a marriage of convenience but the shameful, shambolic events of the 2005 United States Grand Prix may well have brought divorce a step closer.

The cause of the unsavoury episode that made unwanted headlines around the world was the high-banked Turn 13 at the Indianapolis Motor Speedway, the latest home of the US Grand Prix. Taken at 200mph (321.9km/h), Turn 13 is a corner unique to modern F1 racing and one which places such demands on the car that it can create abnormal tyre wear. Alarm bells began ringing on Friday practice when Ralf Schumacher slammed his Toyota into the wall on the Turn 13 banking – exactly the same spot where he had injured his back in the course of the previous year's race. Left-rear tyre failure was held responsible and, with other teams running on Michelin tyres also suffering accidents during practice, the French company announced that those tyres were unsafe for extended high-speed use on Turn 13. It flew in another set from its Clermont-Ferrand headquarters but, when tested, these had the same problem. Michelin was forced to admit that it could not guarantee the safety

of its tyres at Indianapolis. With seven of the ten teams –
McLaren, Renault, Williams, Sauber, Toyota, BAR and Red
Bull – running on Michelins, the outlook was bleak.

On the morning of the race, Ecclestone and circuit owner
Tony George tried to gain approval for a chicane to be
inserted at Turn 13, thereby forcing the cars to slow down
to a safer speed, but Ferrari – one of the three teams on
Bridgestone tyres – refused to entertain the proposition.
Furthermore, the FIA rejected any efforts to alter the circuit,
even though the Michelin teams had offered to sacrifice all
points scored in the race. The FIA stated: 'To change the
course to help some of the teams would be grossly unfair
to those teams which have come to Indianapolis with the
correct tyres.'

The 120,000 spectators remained largely oblivious to
the behind-the-scenes controversy and when all twenty
cars lined up on the grid – with Jarno Trulli's Toyota on
pole – it seemed as if they were about to witness a normal
Grand Prix. The twenty set off on the usual parade lap,
but as they approached the final turn – Turn 13 – the 14
Michelin runners peeled off into the pit lane, leaving just
the six Bridgestone cars to start the race. Ferrari's Michael
Schumacher, who had been fifth fastest, now found himself
on pole, with team-mate Rubens Barrichello behind. There
was then the bizarre spectacle of five empty rows until the
Jordans and Minardis made up the numbers.

The crowd responded to the Michelin withdrawal with a
chorus of boos. Objects were thrown on to the track and
some spectators went home in protest. Several TV stations
dropped their coverage. Their viewers didn't miss much. A
field of two Ferraris and, as one observer put it, 'four cars
making a noise', was never going to make for a gripping
spectacle and for probably the first time in F1 history the
roar of the engines was drowned out by the dissent from
the stands.

The Ferraris were embarrassingly superior to their

quartet of rivals from the wrong end of the grid. The only lead changes occurred on lap 26, as Schumacher's slow pit stop enabled Barrichello to take advantage, and on lap 51, when Schumacher, exiting the pit lane, forced Barrichello onto the grass. After that incident, the Ferrari pair were reminded over their radios not to crash out of the race, and both eased into cruise mode over the remaining 22 laps.

Schumacher went on to record his first win of the season, although it still left him 25 points behind Spain's Fernando Alonso in the Drivers' Championship. Barrichello was second with Tiago Monteiro in the Jordan third over a lap behind. It was Monteiro's first podium finish and the first ever by a Portuguese driver. Try telling him that it was a hollow achievement! For the record, the Indian driver Narain Karthikeyan was fourth in the other Jordan with the Minardi duo of Christijan Albers and Patrick Friesacher fifth and sixth. Unusually for a Grand Prix, there were no retirements, but then this had been no usual Grand Prix.

Even the ultra-competitive Schumacher felt uneasy about the manner of his success and most of the F1 world labelled the proceedings a 'farce'. As recriminations flew, Ecclestone raged: 'I'm furious at the stupidity of it all. There should have been a compromise but we could not get one. I tried a million things and thought that if we could get them on the grid we were halfway there. But it did not happen. We were just starting to build a great image in America on TV and with the fans. All that has gone out of the window.'

David Coulthard, whose Red Bull was one of the non-starters, echoed those sentiments. 'The bottom line is Michelin made a mistake. But after that the FIA had it in their hands to find a solution and ensure we all raced out there. The most important people, the fans, have been forgotten in all of this. It is them I feel sorry for. This is going to leave a long-lasting bitter taste in people's mouths. Quite frankly, as a driver, I'm embarrassed to be involved in this situation. It's a very sad day for racing.'

The seven teams who pulled out of the US Grand Prix were initially found guilty by the FIA World Motor Sport Council of failing to ensure they had suitable tyres and of wrongfully refusing to start the race, but the verdict was later overturned.

In a bid to restore public confidence in the brand, Michelin offered to reimburse fans who had bought tickets, but the damage to Formula One's reputation in America may ultimately prove beyond repair. The divorce lawyers are circling.

FORTY-ONE PEOPLE WENT TO MOW

BRITISH LAWN MOWER RACING ASSOCIATION 12-HOUR ENDURANCE RACE, 29 JULY 2006

Jim Gavin had raced cars all over the world but by 1973 the Irishman had become disillusioned with the prohibitive cost of the sport. So that year he and a few locals gathered at the Cricketers Arms in Wisborough Green, West Sussex, to try and devise a cheap form of motor sport that was accessible to all. While downing their pints in search of inspiration, they gazed out across the village green and saw a groundsman mowing the cricket pitch. In a Eureka-like moment, they decided that lawn mower racing was the answer, reasoning that everyone had a lawn mower in their garden shed. Soon afterwards, around eighty competitors turned up for the inaugural lawn mower race in a local farmer's field. A new variation of motor sport had arrived on the scene.

The British Lawn Mower Racing Association now boasts some 250 members. The 12-date race calendar starts in May and ends in October and includes the British Grand Prix as well as the jewel in the crown of lawn mower racing, the 12-Hour Endurance Race. Although for many competitors the social drinking is as important as the racing (actor Oliver Reed, who lived nearby and was the possessor of a legendary thirst, regularly entered a team), lawn mower racing has also attracted more conventional racers. Stirling Moss has won both the British Grand Prix and the 12-Hour Race while five times Le Mans winner Derek Bell has won the 12-Hour

Race twice, once in tandem with Moss. Discovering that they were up against a team of Stirling Moss and Derek Bell, it is little wonder that the other entrants needed a stiff drink.

The competing mowers are split into four classes according to design and the degree of modification. There used to be a fifth class until hand-mowers, with the driver running along behind, were wisely banned on safety grounds. Original mower engines are retained on all of the ride-on machines but the blades are removed for obvious reasons.

Since the mid-1980s the 12-Hour Endurance Race has been held in a huge field at Brinsbury College near Pulborough. The bumpy circuit measures ⅘ mile (1.3km) in length and the fastest speeds – of up to 40mph (64.4km/h) – are reached on the 500 yard (457m) long pit straight. The race starts at 8p.m. on the Saturday with the drivers making a Le Mans-style dash across the track and finishes at 8a.m. on the Sunday. Each team is allowed up to three drivers (all competitors must be over 18), who tend to operate in 30-minute shifts. Basic floodlights illuminate the main straight during the hours of darkness but the rest of the track is lit only by mower headlamps. Not surprisingly, in the dead of the Sussex night driver error is commonplace.

Forty-one teams, including one from Luxembourg, lined up for the 2006 event, fielding names such as Pain in the Grass Racing, Crash Test Dummies and The 24-Inch Boys. Among them were three all-women teams – Mower Maids, The Boozy Birds and Bad Girls. While a number of competitors fell by the wayside on the hard, unforgiving ground (six mowers sustained broken axles), Accident Prone, under the tutorship of local mechanic Jeremy Eldridge, powered to victory, completing 366 laps to finish 26 ahead of their nearest rivals, Northerners Kick Grass. The result was scarcely a surprise. Accident Prone's mower was the same machine that had triumphed in 2005.

This was clearly the Arkle of lawn mowers. It had travelled nearly 300 miles (483km) at an average speed of 31⅕mph (50.2km/h), compared to The Boozy Birds (winners of the unmodified Class 1) who pottered around at a more sedate 9mph (14.5km/h).

The for-lawn competitors soon adjourned to the pub to recount and embellish their tales of derring-do. By the time the alcohol had dulled their aches and pains, most were vowing that nothing would stop them coming back to mow next year.

A PASSAGE THROUGH INDIA

THE INDIAN AUTORICKSHAW CHALLENGE, 21–27 AUGUST 2006

The people of India have long grown accustomed to witnessing strange and colourful sights on their streets. But few can have been as bizarre as the first Indian Autorickshaw Challenge, in which 16 teams raced their brightly decorated vehicles 620 miles (998km) from Chennai to Kanyakumari, the southern-most tip of the country … just for fun.

The challenge was the idea of Aravind Kumar who had taken part in the 2005 Budapest-Bamako Rally, a gruelling adventure road race. He decided to come up with a race in which participants would be 'making their way through monsoon rains, crowds, variable road conditions, and other typically Indian obstacles'. Instead of cars, he alighted upon the autorickshaw, India's 'national vehicle'. He explained: 'There are Indians who own many Mercedes cars. There are Indians who do not even have a bicycle. But every Indian would have travelled in an autorickshaw at least once in his or her lifetime.' However, only three of the teams were actually Indian; the rest, from as far afield as Britain, the United States, Hungary, Armenia and Russia, had never even seen, let alone driven, an autorickshaw before. Helpfully the organisers arranged a crash course – although some drivers took the invitation literally.

For the uninitiated, an autorickshaw seats three people, has three wheels, a single cylinder, two-stroke engine, five gears, an average cruising speed of 35mph (56.3km/h) and a top speed of 50mph (80.5km/h). It is kick started. In western terms, it is not dissimilar to a souped-up milk float, although one competitor likened it to a motorised eggshell.

Each team paid €1,500 to enter the race, in return for which they were provided with an autorickshaw and an escort throughout the event to undertake any repairs and help them if they became hopelessly lost. At the end the vehicles were sold and the proceeds donated to charity.

Hundreds of locals turned out to watch as the teams – with names like Curry in a Hurry, Tamil Devils and Riska Miska – set off from the beach in Chennai on the morning of 21 August. Some vehicles were decorated with go faster stripes and flags but Team Armageddon from Russia outdid everyone by equipping theirs with a surround sound system and refrigerator. As early as day two, Tamil Devils and Riska Miska collided but were able to continue after hasty repairs. Autorickshaws may be relatively easy to repair but they are not built to withstand major collisions. As one competitor put it: 'The only thing you can risk hitting in a rickshaw is a goat or a chicken and even then the odds are it will take off and roll over.'

There were regular fuel stops en route, which often required the services of four attendants – one to pour the fuel in, one to measure out the oil (the rickshaws don't have oil pumps), one to count out the money and one to ask the driver to take his photo. If the oil wasn't mixed properly, the vehicle tended to splutter to a halt half a mile (0.8km) down the road. Eventually the teams learned that the trick during refuelling was to rock the rickshaws violently from side to side, thereby mixing the fuel. They had also been warned of the danger of 'jumpers' – villagers who throw themselves in front of tourist vehicles in the hope that they will be sufficiently injured to earn sympathy money … but not so badly that their family will need to pay for a funeral.

Finally after seven days, various crashes, calamities and engine changes, the competitors reached their destination of Kanyakumari. Despite breaking down on the opening day, team Pukka Tuk Tuk – piloted by Ian and Rachel Bayles, a British couple from Goa – were declared the world's first autorickshaw champions. There was no prize, just the satisfaction of having taken part in a glorious adventure that harks back to the very birth of motor sport.

THE DELIBERATE CRASH
SINGAPORE GRAND PRIX,
28 SEPTEMBER 2008

The 2008 Singapore Grand Prix was the first-ever Formula One night race, but instead it would be chiefly remembered for one of the sport's biggest scandals, whereby the Renault team deliberately engineered a crash so that their other driver could have a better chance of winning the race.

Coming into the fifteenth race of the season (with three to go), Britain's Lewis Hamilton led the Drivers' Championship by a point from Brazilian Felipe Massa, with Fernando Alonso's Renault down in seventh. Renault had not won a race for nearly two years and were rumoured to be considering quitting the sport. Massa started on pole in Singapore with Hamilton second and Alonso only fifteenth. Massa led around the street circuit from Hamilton and Finland's Kimi Raikkonen, the reigning world champion, until, on lap 14, Alonso's Renault team-mate, Nelson Piquet Jr, crashed into the circuit wall at Turn 17, necessitating the deployment of the safety car. Alonso had stopped surprisingly early (on lap 12) for fuel and tyres, rejoining at the back of the field, but as many of the drivers ahead of him pitted under the safety car, Alonso found himself promoted up to fifth. Massa's cause was not helped when Ferrari released him prematurely from the pits, not only into the path of Adrian Sutil's Force India but also with the fuel hose still attached to his car. Massa stopped just before the pit-lane exit, hotly pursued by Ferrari mechanics.

To add to his misery, he was subsequently given a drive-through penalty for an unsafe release from the pits and was relegated to last place. After various other penalties were served and pit stops taken, Alonso moved into the lead and, despite making his second pit stop on lap 42, he held on to win from Nico Rosberg's Williams and Hamilton's McLaren. It was Alonso's first victory of the season. Piquet described his crash as a simple mistake, and nobody, apart from a few cynics, really thought anything more about it. Freelance Formula One journalist Joe Saward dismissed these conspiracy theories, writing: 'One likes to believe that no team would ever be so desperate as to have a driver throw his car at a wall.'

As the son of a three-times world champion, great things had been expected of Piquet but the young Brazilian had struggled for much of the season, and so it was a surprise to many when he kept his Renault seat for 2009. His fortunes did not improve, however, and in August 2009, without a single championship point to his name that year, he confirmed that he had been dropped by the team. He immediately hit out at Renault team boss Flavio Briatore and sensationally claimed that Briatore and experienced engineer Pat Symonds had asked him to stage the Singapore crash deliberately in order to help Alonso.

The sport's governing body, the FIA, charged Renault with conspiracy and race fixing, whereupon Renault counter-accused Piquet of making false allegations and blackmail. Then Renault had a sudden change of heart, announcing that they would not contest the charges after all and that Briatore and Symonds had left the team. The 'Crashgate' hearing, as it was dubbed in the press, took place in September 2009. Symonds confessed to his role in the conspiracy and expressed his 'eternal regret and shame', blaming his actions on 'a misguided devotion to my team'. Briatore continued to deny involvement but an unnamed Renault employee, Witness X, testified that the flamboyant

Italian knew about the scheme. The FIA found that Alonso had no knowledge of the planned crash.

Briatore and Symonds received bans, but these were subsequently overturned by a French court, although both agreed not to work in Formula One for a specific time. In 2011, Symonds returned to F1 as a consultant for Virgin Racing and two years later was appointed Chief Technical Officer with the Williams team. In 2010, Renault apologised unreservedly to Piquet and his father for defaming them. So ended one of F1's messiest sagas.

FINAL TURN DECIDER
BRAZILIAN GRAND PRIX,
2 NOVEMBER 2008

The 2008 Formula One World Drivers' Championship ended in the most dramatic manner imaginable. It was not only decided in the last race, on the last lap, but on the very last corner – and while it brought heartache to Felipe Massa in front of his home crowd, it handed a first title to Lewis Hamilton.

Heading into the final race at Interlagos, Hamilton held a healthy seven-point lead over Massa, but the Brazilian put his Ferrari on pole (Hamilton was down in fourth) and with heavy rain forecast anything could happen. If Massa were to pick up ten points for first place, Hamilton needed to finish fifth in order to clinch the title. If Hamilton finished sixth, their points totals would be tied, but Massa would claim the title on a count-back by virtue of having more victories.

In a hint of what was to come, a downpour four minutes before the scheduled race time delayed the start by ten minutes and forced the drivers to switch to intermediate tyres. When the race did get under way, Massa retained his lead but with conditions still treacherous, accidents involving David Coulthard – forcing him to retire on the first lap of his last Grand Prix – and Nelson Piquet Jr, meant that the safety car had to be brought out until lap five. As track conditions steadily improved, drivers began to switch to dry-weather tyres but this merely served to underline Massa's superiority. By lap 54 of the 71, he led

Fernando Alonso by over nine seconds with Ferrari team-mate Kimi Raikkonen in third and Hamilton in fourth, still on course for the title but being caught rapidly by Sebastian Vettel's Toro Rosso. Then on lap 63, light rain began to fall, and most of the drivers pitted for intermediate tyres. An exception was Toyota's Timo Glock who opted to remain on dry-weather tyres in the hope that the rain would soon pass. The team's decision to stay out elevated the German from seventh to fourth as those ahead of him pitted. Suddenly Hamilton was looking vulnerable.

On lap 69 – just two from the finish – the rain became heavier and Hamilton ran wide, allowing Vettel to snatch fifth place. When Massa took the chequered flag, Hamilton was down in sixth. The Ferrari team celebrated wildly, certain that their man had won the title, but their joy was to be short-lived. Even on dry tyres, Glock had raced competitively on the wet track until, on the final lap, he struggled badly for grip. Approaching the final corner just a couple of hundred yards from the flag, he was off line and had slowed to a crawl, enabling Hamilton to pass him and snatch fifth place and the world title by a single point. Such was the chaos that Hamilton did not know that he had done enough until his team told him over the radio. Massa had been world champion for 30 seconds. The outcome was so unbelievable that a Hollywood screenwriter would have dismissed it as too far-fetched.

As conspiracy theories circulated, Glock defended himself. 'I had no chance to resist the guys on intermediate tyres because they were just so much quicker. I had to stay off the racing line because there was so much tyre rubber on it, which becomes incredibly slippery in the wet. I don't know how anyone can think I just pulled over. If Lewis had not overtaken me in that corner, he would have overtaken me on the following straight because there was no way I could go flat out on the dry tyres.'

So the title had been snatched from the popular Massa in

the cruellest fashion. He has always had more than his fair share of bad luck in Formula One, and how he must have reflected back to Singapore and his team's costly fuel hose blunder, which had turned a likely ten points into zero.

LAST TO FIRST

CANADIAN GRAND PRIX, 12 JUNE 2011

Not many drivers can say they won a Grand Prix after being last at over halfway, let alone having also been involved in two accidents and sustained a drive-through penalty during the race. Then again, the 2011 Canadian Grand Prix in Montreal was no ordinary race. From start to finish it ran for over four hours after racing was suspended for more than two hours partway through because of torrential rain. Once again rain equalled high drama in Formula One.

Runaway championship leader, Sebastian Vettel, put his Red Bull on pole ahead of the Ferraris of Fernando Alonso and Felipe Massa with Vettel's team-mate, Mark Webber, in fourth. The British McLaren pairing of Lewis Hamilton and Jenson Button lined up fifth and seventh respectively. The race began behind the safety car, and once the action got under way for real on lap five, Hamilton and Webber immediately collided, relegating them to seventh and fourteenth. Three laps later, Hamilton, anxious to make up lost ground, tried to overtake his team-mate but the two came together and Hamilton hit the pit wall, forcing his retirement and the deployment of the safety car. Button was able to continue, but was given a drive-through penalty for speeding behind the safety car, and when he rejoined the race he was down in fifteenth. On lap 20 of the scheduled 70 laps, and with Vettel holding a commanding lead, another rainstorm made the Circuit Gilles Villeneuve so dangerous that the race was suspended. At that stage the chances of it ever being resumed looked as gloomy as the skies overhead.

Eventually the rain eased and the race was restarted behind the safety car with Vettel leading and Button down in tenth place. When the safety car came in, the circuit had dried out sufficiently for the drivers to change from full wet tyres to intermediates. Button did so on lap 36 but on exiting the pit lane, he tried to pass Alonso at Turn Three, the two cars touched and the Ferrari spun and beached, bringing out the safety car once more. Button was left with a puncture and after heading to the pits he found himself in twenty-first and last place. It seemed his day was over.

But the 2009 world champion was not one to give up without a fight and by lap 44 he had worked his way back up to fourteenth. Soon he was in the points and then, after more new tyres, he was up to fourth behind Vettel, Michael Schumacher's Mercedes and Webber. A sixth safety car – following a collision between Nick Heidfeld's Renault and Kamui Kobayashi's Sauber – compacted the field and Button, now a man on a mission, managed to pass Webber and Schumacher on the same lap to move up to second. Vettel led him by 0.9 seconds starting the final lap, but, feeling the pressure for once, the reigning world champion ran wide at Turn Six and Button needed no second invitation. Button went on to crown his amazing comeback by taking the chequered flag for what he described as the best win of his career. Neither Hamilton nor Alonso attached any blame to Button for the accidents, with Hamilton generously hailing his team-mate's drive as 'utterly fantastic'.

McLaren team principal Martin Whitmarsh echoed those sentiments. 'I think it was one of the best wins in the history of F1. From twenty-first I don't know how many times he had to overtake people. This was 90 per cent him and 10 per cent the car. He did a great, great, great job.' Vettel went on to take his second successive world title, but there was little doubt that Button's was the drive of the season.

THIS LITTLE PIGGY
PIG-N-FORD WORLD CHAMPIONSHIPS, 9 AUGUST 2014

Since 1925, the Tillamook County Fair in Oregon, USA, has staged a curious event in which drivers race around a dirt track at the wheel of a stripped-down Model T Ford while carrying a live 20lb (9.1kg) pig under one arm. Following a series of elimination heats, five cars take part in the final and line up on the start line with their engines off. The drivers stand next to the grandstands, and when the starting pistol fires, they run across to the pig pen, grab a young pig, hand-crank their car and set off around the track. At the end of the lap, they stop, turn off the engine, pick up a different pig, and race another lap. The first driver to complete three laps in this manner – without losing their pig – is declared the winner. The average winning time is a little over a minute per lap. The victorious driver receives a trophy; the victorious pigs go away only with memories.

The idea for the race came about back in the early 1920s when a local man driving a Model T Ford saw a neighbour's pig running loose, chased it down in the car and scooped it up. The story captured people's imagination and they decided to turn it into an annual event.

Technique is key, particularly when deciding whether to hold the pig face up or face down in the car. 'They like to poop a lot,' warns driver John Haertel, 'so you get some of that on your car. They feed them pretty good.' It is also helpful to find a relaxed pig if possible. Before selecting a pig from the pen, fellow driver Marty Walker pokes them and grabs 'whichever one doesn't freak out'. Everybody stresses that the pigs are treated humanely.

Walker is very much the Michael Schumacher of Pig-N-Ford racing. He has hogged the limelight since the 1990s, racking up over a dozen wins, although he was sensationally disqualified in 2010 in what became known as the Great Camshaft Controversy. In 2014, he lost his crown to Ben Salo.

Bernie Ecclestone is always said to be looking for ways of brightening up Formula One, so maybe the introduction of a squealing, wriggling pig into the driver's cockpit could be the answer. Let's see how fast Lewis Hamilton can go around Monaco carrying a live porker.

A CRAZY MISCALCULATION
MONACO GRAND PRIX, 24 MAY 2015

The Mercedes team hardly put a foot wrong in steering Lewis Hamilton to a third Formula One World Championship title in 2015, but they did manage to blunder big time in Monaco where, by virtue of an unscheduled, unnecessary, late pit stop, they contrived to snatch defeat from the jaws of certain victory. Ironically, ahead of the race, Mercedes announced they had extended their contract with Hamilton until the end of 2018. In the wake of the Monaco fiasco, Hamilton could have been forgiven for briefly wondering if there was a get-out clause.

Up until lap 64 of 78, it had all been business as usual. After qualifying on pole, Hamilton led from the start, and went on to establish a lead of almost 20 seconds over his team-mate Nico Rosberg and Ferrari's Sebastian Vettel. Then 17-year-old Max Verstappen – the youngest driver in F1 history – crashed his Toro Rosso into the back of Romain Grosjean's Lotus at Sainte Devote, bringing out the safety car. Hamilton was quickly pitted over a minor concern about the heat in his tyres, the Mercedes team convinced that they could return him to the action ahead of his pursuers. However, they had miscalculated badly, and Hamilton emerged from the pits in third place behind Rosberg and Vettel. As race leader, Hamilton had caught up with the safety car on his in-lap quicker than his rivals and so had lost more time than them on his way into the pits. Making a split-second decision to bring Hamilton in, Mercedes had not factored those lost seconds into the equation. The safety car was withdrawn on lap 70, but with overtaking at Monaco notoriously difficult, Rosberg was able to win unchallenged leaving Hamilton, stuck behind Vettel, a frustrated third.

Mercedes team boss Toto Wolff admitted after the race: 'We got our numbers wrong. We thought we had the gap for Lewis to take fresh tyres and come back out in the lead behind the safety car, ahead of Nico and covering any risk of another competitor taking fresh tyres. But the calculation was incorrect.'

In the past, Hamilton had not always dealt well with adversity but on this occasion he was surprisingly philosophical. It was probably because he knew he was driving for the best team and that they would do their utmost to make up for their uncharacteristic slip. He was to be proved right.